2ⁿᵈ edition

masterMind

Workbook

Chris Valvona
Lindsay Warwick

Concept development:
Mariela Gil Vierma

Level 2

Macmillan Education
4 Crinan Street
London N1 9XW
A division of Macmillan Publishers Limited

Companies and representatives throughout the world

ISBN 9780230469853 with key
ISBN 9780230469860 without key

This edition published 2015
First edition published 2010

Designed by emc design limited
Cover design by Tony Richardson, Wooden Ark Ltd.
Cover photograph courtesy of Getty Images/Anna Bryukhanova.

Picture research by Victoria Gaunt

The authors would like to thank the schools, teachers, and
students whose input has been invaluable in preparing this new
edition. They would also like to thank the editorial and design
teams at Macmillan for doing such a great job of organizing the
material and bringing it to life.

The publishers would like to thank the following educators
and institutions who reviewed materials and provided us
with invaluable insight and feedback for the development of
masterMind 2nd edition:

Isidro Almedarez, Deniz Atesok, Monica Delgadillo, Elaine
Hodgson, Mark Lloyd, Rufus Vaughan-Spruce, Kristof van Houdt,
Rob Duncan, James Conboy, Jonathan Danby, Fiona Craig, Martin
Guilfoyle, Rodrigo Rosa.

The authors and publishers would like to thank the following for
permission to reproduce the following material.

Extract from 'The best things in life are free' by Charles
Leadbeater © New Statesman 2014, first published in New
Statesman 15 January 2010. Reprinted by permission of the
publisher. www.newstatesman.com, Extract from 'I've swapped
my paper clip for a house' by David Leafe © Telegraph Group
Limited 2014, first published in the Daily Telegraph 19 April 2006.
Reprinted by permission of the publisher. www.telegraph.co.uk,
Extract from 'The animals and plants we cannot live without' by
Richard Gray © Telegraph Group Limited 2014, first published in
the Daily Telegraph 15 November 2008. Reprinted by permission
of the publisher. www.telegraph.co.uk, Extract from 'Popular brain
training games do not make users any smarter' by Kate Devlin
© Telegraph Group Limited 2014, first published in the Daily
Telegraph 21 April 2010. Reprinted by permission of the publisher.
www.telegraph.co.uk, Extract from 'New study says people still
don't understand their online lives can cost them their real jobs'
by Kate Knibbs, first published 03 June 2013. Reprinted from
www.digitaltrends.com with permission. © 2014 Designtechnica
Corporation dba Digital Trends. All rights reserved, Extract from
'15 ways supermarkets trick you into spending more money'
by Gus Lubin © Business Insider Inc. 2014, first published in
Business Insider 26 July 2011. Reprinted by permission of the
publisher. www.businessinsider.com, Extract from 'Being a
conscious consumer need not consume you' by Gia Machlin ©
Gia Machlin 2014, first published in Ecoplum 25 September 2013.
Reprinted here with permission. www.ecoplum.com, Extract from
'The Importance of Play for adults' by Margarita Tartakovsky
© Copyright 2014 Psych Central.com. All rights reserved.
Reprinted here with permission. http://psychcentral.com/blog/
archives/2012/11/15/the-importance-of-play-for-adults/
Extract from 'Why is vinyl becoming popular' by Lucas Kiss
© Reawaken Media LLC 2014, first published in Techgeek
15 August 2013. Reprinted by permission of the publisher.
www.techgeek.com.au, Extract from 'Robot to expose hidden
meanings of pyramids' originally published on TechNews Daily 12

August 2010. Reprinted with permission. www.technewsdaily.com
Extract from 'How to make money busking' by Thursday Bram.
Originally published on Investopedia 12 December 2012.
www.investopedia.com

The authors and publishers would like to thank the following for
permission to reproduce their photographs:

Alamy/Bon Appetit pp5, 63, Alamy/The Marsden Archive p60,
Alamy/The Print Collector p46(r), Alamy/Craig Ellenwood p71(b),
Alamy/JTB MEDIA CREATION, Inc p71(t), Alamy/Sioen Gérard
p74(d), Alamy/Blaine Harrington III p74(b), Alamy/imageBROKER
p72, Alamy/Juice Images p45, Alamy/jvphoto p21, Alamy/
David Noton Photography p74(c), Alamy/PhotoAlto sas p71(c),
Alamy/Joshua Rainey p23, Alamy/Kevin Schafer p70, Alamy/Neil
Setchfield p73, Alamy/Shotshop GmbH p17, Alamy/Olaf Speier
p7, Alamy/Stocktrek Images, Inc p14, Alamy/Jochen Tack p40,
Alamy/Tetra Images p54(t), Alamy/komkrit tonusin p33, Alamy/
UpperCut Images p42; **Corbis**/Blutgruppe p36, Corbis/John
Burcham/National Geographic Society p74(e), Corbis/Richard
Crisp/SuperStock p12, Corbis/Zero Creatives p24, Corbis/237/
Robert Daly/Ocean p56(b), Corbis/Kevin Dodge p54(b), Corbis/
Monalyn Gracia p64, Corbis/Troy House p19, Corbis/Hero Images
p26,Corbis/Sean Justice p6, Corbis/Tim Pannell p65, Corbis/
Paul Simcock/Blend Images p52, Corbis/ Image Source p56(t);
Digital Vision p15; **FLPA**/IMAGEBROKER,CHRISTIAN HÜTTER/
Imagebroker p31, FLPA/Imagebroker p29, FLPA/Chris Mattison
p30; **Getty Images** p39, Getty Images/Archive Photos p46(l),
Getty Images/Yuri Arcurs p22,Getty Images/Andy Crawford p34,
Getty Images/AFP Creative p74(g), Getty Images/Tim Flach p11,
Getty Images/franckreporter p55, Getty Images/Lynn Harris - The
Little Red Hen p69, Getty Images/Gavriel Jecan p74(a), Getty
Images/Michel Mako p47, Getty Images/Sherwin McGehee p4,
Getty Images/Denver Post p38, Getty Images/Gamma-Rapho
p8, Getty Images/Mint Images/Tim Robbins p43(b), Getty Images/
Greg Schneider/birdphotographer.ca p28, Getty Images/Oli Scarff/
Staff p48, Getty Images/Henrik Sorensen p49, Getty Images/
Jane Sweeney p74(f),Getty Images/UIG pp13(t,b), 50, Getty
Images/Andrew Bret Wallis p18; **Glow Images**/Imagesource
p53(t); **ImageSource** pp9, 20; **Science Photo Library**/MASSIMO
BREGA, THE LIGHTHOUSE p35, Science Photo Library/
CLAUDE NURIDSANY & MARIE PERENNOU p32, Science Photo
Library/ DETLEV VAN RAVENSWAAY p10; **REX Features**/Everett
Collection p66, REX/Denis Closon p44; **Thinkstock**/Hemera
p43(t), Thinkstock/istock pp37, 51, 53(b), 58(b), 58(t), 61, 62(l,r),
Thinkstock/moodboard p27.

Printed and bound in Thailand

2018 2017 2016 2015
10 9 8 7 6 5 4 3 2 1

CONTENTS

UNIT 1 MONEY-FREE

1 READING: text organization

A Read the article. Underline the main idea in each paragraph.

THE BEST THINGS IN LIFE ARE free

Why do we care so much about money? What we value most—love, dignity, good conduct, pride, trust, friendship, care—does not come from money. If we were to try to use it to buy any of these things, most people would think we were crazy. Imagine, for example, asking, "How much do I owe you for that?" after a friend gives you advice. Those aspects of our lives that we really cherish are so valuable because they do not have a price attached. Poets do not write for stock options. Good relationships do not need insurance policies. People do not need incentives to love each other.

Not surprisingly, most utopias were planned to succeed without money. Yet societies that went without it inevitably failed. Cities have functioned without money, but usually only in extreme circumstances, such as war, when gold, ammunition, and food became the currency. Closer to home, experiments such as time banks (which have attempted to use time as a currency) and local economic trading schemes have been talked about rather than implemented.

The problem is what we value in itself and what we put a price on are often inextricably linked. My wife and I fell in love over a series of lunches in London restaurants—yet you will not find "falling in love" listed on the bill after the sparkling water. The paid-for meals were simply a way of expressing our love, which is beyond price. The value something has in itself is often "hidden" behind the entrance ticket we buy to make it possible. The cover price of a great book never captures its value.

The objects in our lives that we really value—the stuff we cannot bear to throw away—mark out relationships that we value: a memento from a vacation, a picture from a wedding, and toys kept from childhood. That is one reason we are so fascinated and consumed by homes, because they sustain relationships. It is also why we pay to be part of huge social gatherings—festivals, carnivals, sporting events: these are all mass shows of emotion that give us a sense of being caught up in something that is bigger than ourselves.

Adapted from www.newstatesman.com

B Read the article in Exercise A again. Choose two examples in each paragraph that support the main idea.

C Read the article in Exercise A again. Choose T (true), F (false), or NM (not mentioned) for each statement.

1 The author believes that certain things cannot be bought with money.   *T / F / NM*
2 In his opinion, societies should function without money.   *T / F / NM*
3 It is possible to separate the value of something and the price we pay.   *T / F / NM*
4 Being at a big event makes us think we are involved in something important.   *T / F / NM*

2 VOCABULARY: consumerism and sustainability

Complete the forum comment with the correct form of the words from the box.

> barter   consume   dumpster   factory farming
> forage   livelihood   sustainable   sweatshop

HOME | FORUMS | NEWS | ADVICE   SEARCH

GREEN TALK

My Green Adventure
by AnyaB on January 2 at 10:04 p.m.
My resolution for the next 12 months is to lead a more ethical and (1) _____ life. Here's what I
plan to do:
I'll only buy the food and drink that I know I'll (2) _____ so that I don't waste anything in my
refrigerator. This means I'll need a shopping list! I'll go to the woods to (3) _____ for berries
so I can make my own jam and then I'll (4) _____ it for some of my neighbor's homemade
produce (leaving some for myself, of course). I'll avoid food that comes from (5) _____
and instead support the (6) _____ of local, ethical farmers. I'll avoid buying clothes made
in (7) _____ and instead try and make my own. I'll also look for unwanted furniture in
(8) _____ rather than buy anything new.
So, here goes. Wish me luck!

3 GRAMMAR: adverb phrases

A Match the type of adverb phrase (1–5) to the examples (a–e).
Underline the example of the type of adverb phrase in each case.

1	time	a)	People exchange goods in order to save money.
2	frequency	b)	A large amount of bartering is done online.
3	place	c)	Freecycle has become more popular in recent times.
4	manner	d)	Some people barter on a daily basis.
5	purpose	e)	We use fewer resources by exchanging things with each other.

B Complete the advertisement with the phrases (a–h).

a)	across the country	e)	on our Events page
b)	by looking for	f)	on the final weekend of each month
c)	next Saturday	g)	through a traditional barter system
d)	on a regular basis	h)	to fill your cupboards

swapyourgoods.com

HOME | Register | Login | Events | Ideas | FAQs

Making your own produce is a rewarding experience so why not share
your rewards with others? We at *swapyourgoods.com* organize events
(1) ____, where you can trade your homemade goods. Not only do you get
to meet and exchange ideas with people (2) ____, you can also take home
a variety of products (3) ____. Everything is done (4) ____, which means no
money is required and things couldn't be simpler. You can find out more
(5) ____ the name of your neighborhood (6) ____. We hold events (7) ____,
which means our next swap will be held (8) ____.

4 VOCABULARY: describing used items

A Complete the tips for buying used items with the words from the box.

| condition   drop off   in good working order   second-hand   throw in   up for grabs |

1. If the price is too high, ask the seller to _____ something free of charge.
2. Ask the seller to _____ it _____ at your house if they're passing through your neighborhood.
3. Always check the _____ of the item and make sure any machinery is _____. You can't complain after the sale.
4. If something good is _____, call quickly or you might miss out.
5. Keep an eye out for rare _____ items. You never know, they might be worth something.

WATCH OUT!

✗ I'll throw in it, as an added incentive.

✓ _____, as an added incentive.

B Complete the conversation with the phrases from Exercise A. Include *it* or *them* where appropriate.

Yang: Hi, Joey. I'm calling about the **(1)** _____ desk. Is it still for sale?

Joey: Yeah, it is. By the way, if you still want the chair that goes with it, I could **(2)** _____, too. You know, as an added incentive.

Yang: Wow! Thanks, that's really nice. And another thing, Joey … is the desk lamp still **(3)** _____? I'd like that, too. Is it **(4)** _____?

Joey: Yeah, no one bought it. And it works fine; it's in really good **(5)** _____, actually. But I'm asking $10 for that.

Yang: Oh, I see. Maybe I'll leave it, then.

Joey: OK, so you're taking two things, right? Would you like me to **(6)** _____ at your apartment?

Yang: Oh, I'd really appreciate that. I don't have any transportation yet.

5 COMMUNICATION STRATEGY: hedging

A 🔊 01 Listen to the conversation. Choose the correct option to complete the sentences.

1. Mike's *eager / reluctant* to organize a clothes swapping party.
2. Claire presents her opinions *politely / forcefully*.
3. Mike *agrees / doesn't agree* to host the party.

B Complete the sentences with the phrases from the box.

argue that   guess   more or less   pretty sure   seems to me   tend to think

1 Well, I _____ it's an OK idea.
2 I'd _____ it's more than OK. It's great!
3 I'm _____ some people will just bring dirty, old clothes.
4 Oh, I _____ people are a bit better than that.
5 I went to a similar party last year and thought the clothes were _____ in excellent condition.
6 It _____ you're not convinced.

C Listen again and check your answers.

6 GRAMMAR: negative questions

Complete the questions with a negative auxiliary word. Complete the responses with *yes* or *no*.

1 **A:** I'm not quite sure what happens at a clothes swapping party.
   B: Oh, _____ you been to one before? I thought you had.
   A: _____, it's my first time.
2 **A:** Why are you giving away this dress? _____ you want to keep it for a special occasion?
   B: _____, I'm bored with it these days.
3 **A:** I'm hoping to swap this jacket for a new coat.
   B: _____ it too warm for a coat at the moment?
   C: _____, but I'm thinking ahead to the winter.
4 **A:** What's wrong with this t-shirt? _____ it fit you anymore?
   B: _____, it's too tight.
5 **A:** If we want everyone to see the clothes we've brought, _____ we hang them up somewhere?
   B: _____, good idea.
6 **A:** I like the color of this shirt. _____ you buy one like this last month?
   B: _____, mine was much darker.

WATCH OUT!

ⓧ A: Haven't you got enough clothes?
  B: Yes, I've.

✓ A: Haven't you got enough clothes?
  B: Yes, _____.

skillsStudio

A Read the article on page 9. Make inferences. Choose T (true) or F (false).

1 The Internet played a key role in Kyle MacDonald's initial success.   *T / F*
2 He considers his bartering experiment to be unusual.   *T / F*
3 His bartering will now stop.   *T / F*

B Read the article again and choose the correct meaning of the words from the article.

1 *junk* (line 1)
   a) old, broken or useless things
   b) things of low quality
2 *reminiscing* (line 13)
   a) thinking about enjoyable past experiences
   b) telling someone about a difficult situation
3 *glanced* (line 15)
   a) read something quickly and not carefully
   b) looked somewhere quickly

4 *genuinely* (line 32)
   a) honestly, in a sincere way
   b) real, rather than pretend or false
5 *promising* (line 37)
   a) likely to be successful or very good
   b) willing to do something
6 *down-to-earth* (lines 39–40)
   a) mature and logical with no creativity
   b) practical and sensible with no pretensions

C Read the article again and choose the correct options to complete the sentences.

1 The writer says that at the start of the project, the aim appeared to be …
   a) achievable.
   b) worthless.
   c) inspiring.
   d) mad.
2 Kyle MacDonald's aim was to …
   a) have a laugh.
   b) move home.
   c) travel the globe.
   d) start a business.
3 Kyle MacDonald got the idea from …
   a) a childhood activity.
   b) the internet.
   c) a family friend.
   d) a job he once had.
4 Kyle MacDonald's first trade wasn't …
   a) particularly surprising.
   b) especially noteworthy.
   c) a time-consuming process.
   d) conducted over the internet.
5 Kyle MacDonald swapped with people who …
   a) exchanged high value goods.
   b) supported his online project.
   c) were trustworthy.
   d) met him while travelling.
6 Yahk is a place that Kyle MacDonald …
   a) was hoping to visit.
   b) had been to before.
   c) wanted to avoid.
   d) had seen on TV.

7 Kyle MacDonald …
   a) predicted his success.
   b) moved to Yahk.
   c) exceeded his expectations.
   d) continued to barter.

D Imagine Kyle is offering to swap an item you want (e.g., *The Hunger Games* boxset). Write him an email saying why you want this item, and suggest an item that you can offer him in exchange. Say why he should make this exchange with you. Suggest when and where to meet. Write 180–200 words.

News LOCAL

HOME   POLITICS   BUSINESS   CULTURE   ENTERTAINMENT   SPORTS

I've Swapped my Paper Clip for a House ...

Do you, like me, have a drawer somewhere at home full of pieces of **junk** which you've convinced yourself might come in useful some day? If so, the story of Canadian internet entrepreneur, Kyle MacDonald, may inspire you to take a closer look at what hangs around among the leftover screws, lonely rubber bands, and tail-ends of balls of string.

Last July, the 26-year-old former backpacker began, what seemed at the time, a crazy and impossible mission—to
5 trade a single, red paper clip for a house. Advertising this virtually worthless piece of stationery on the internet, he succeeded in swapping it for a series of bigger and better things. This week—nine months and 10 trades later—he announced that his most recent deal has indeed secured him a one-bedroom bungalow in Phoenix, Colorado.

This is all the more remarkable given that MacDonald intended the whole thing to be "just a bit of fun". More hippy than businessman, he is the son of parents who ran a clothing factory in Vancouver. He graduated with a degree in
10 geography from the University of British Colombia before traveling the world doing odd jobs—from delivering pizzas to working on oil rigs.

Unsure of what he wanted to do with his life, he returned to Canada where one day, he received an email from an old friend **reminiscing** about a game called *Bigger and Better*, which they had played as children. This involved starting with small objects and competing to see what they could trade them for.

15 MacDonald finished reading the email, **glanced** down at his desk, and saw a single red paper clip. Why not see what people would give him in exchange for it? And so a bizarre and brilliant idea was born and launched on the web. Alongside a picture of his now much celebrated paper clip, he wrote a humorous statement of his ambitions. "I'm going to keep trading up until I get a house," he wrote. "Or an island. Or a house on an island. You get the idea."

The unspectacular nature of his first trade suggested that he might have a long time to wait. His first offer was a pen in
20 the shape of a fish, which two vegans from Vancouver had discovered on a camping trip. "Being vegans, I guess they wanted very little to do with a fish," said MacDonald. "I had never traded a paper clip with a vegan before, let alone two, so I figured let's do this."

The fish-shaped pen was soon traded for a doorknob featuring a smiley, face and the doorknob, in turn, for an outdoor stove, and then a generator. From the outset, MacDonald insisted on meeting each person with whom he was dealing.
25 It was, he says, "just a great way to meet new people". In this, he had some help. His father, an enthusiastic inventor, had come up with a device to stop wobbly restaurant tables from rocking. MacDonald traveled to trade shows across the U.S. and Canada to promote this device and, along the way, would stop off to meet the people who'd contacted him via his website and with whom he wanted to do business on his paper clip project. "I was doing trades all over the place without spending a cent of my own money on gas or plane fares," he said.

30 As news of the website spread, MacDonald found himself having to choose from among hundreds of offers for each item he advertised, but he says their monetary value was irrelevant. "I only dealt with people I liked the sound of, or who seemed to **genuinely** support the idea of the website."

His dreams of home ownership took a leap forward when a local radio celebrity offered MacDonald a snowmobile. Then, during an appearance on Canadian national TV, he jokingly said that he would travel anywhere in the world to
35 do a deal, except for the unappealing-sounding town of Yahk in British Columbia.

This caused a viewer to offer him a trip to Yahk, which he exchanged for a truck, which he then traded for 30 hours in a Toronto recording studio. Next came the final link in the chain—at least so far. A **promising** young singer offered MacDonald a year's lease on her home in Phoenix in exchange for the studio time.

No one is more surprised by this success than the pleasingly **down-**
40 **to-earth** MacDonald himself. "It's extremely unexpected. People might regard it as an eccentric way to spend your time, but remember that before money was invented, people bartered for centuries." And although MacDonald appears to have achieved his ambition for his humble paper clip, his aim is still to own a home outright.

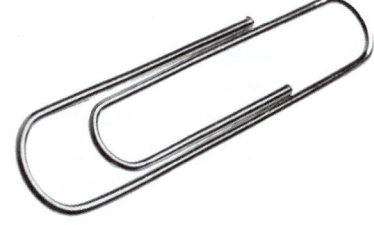

Adapted from www.telegraph.co.uk

UNIT 2 WATCH THIS SPACE ...

1 VOCABULARY: business and innovation

Complete the sentences with the correct form of the words and phrases from the box.

gain a lead   giant   infrastructure   inspire   launch   lobby
press conference   prototype   public relations   rival

1 I work in _____, meaning I control the flow of communication between my company
  and the public.
2 Fresh ideas will be needed if we are to keep up with our many _____.
3 The lack of _____ means it's hard to set up a telecommunications network in some countries.
4 A _____ will be called soon, and the CEO will be expected to announce his retirement.
5 This is just a _____. A model for sale will be produced some time next year.
6 I was so _____ by my first boss that I decided to set up my own business.
7 The internet-based _____ is now valued at $270 billion, even though it started as just
  a small search engine.
8 The company hopes the new technology will help it to _____ in the market.
9 A new smartphone model will be _____ this coming April.
10 We will _____ the politicians until they agree to do what we want.

2 GRAMMAR: future passive

A Choose the correct options to complete the article.

This week, Extreme Travel takes a look at space tourism, which
is fast becoming a very real possibility for more and more people.
For just $250,000, tourists can now book a seat on a shuttle bound
for space. And, those who pay as much as $5 million will
(1) *take* / *be taken* on a four-night all-inclusive trip in a floating space
station. James Hancock has been researching this exciting new type
of "weekend trip" and has more details.

"Space tourism is taking off! From next year, tourists can spend four
nights in a space station with an experienced crew of astronauts.
They will **(2)** *transferred* / *be transferred* to space in a billion-dollar
shuttle, which will then **(3)** *be docking* / *be docked* to the space station.
While in orbit, the tourists will **(4)** *circle* / *be circled* the world every
90 minutes and see 15 sunsets daily. Although there is no gravity in
space, the tourists won't float. They will **(5)** *wear* / *be worn* Velcro suits
which stick to the walls of their pod rooms."

B Find the future passive mistakes in the sentences. Rewrite the sentences correctly.

1 More people could accommodated in the floating hotel in the future.
  _____

2 The plan is to launch the first guests next year, but critics say it may be delaying.
  _____

3 Tourists will be taken to space an expert team of astronauts.
  _____

4 Tourists could be charging up to $5 million for a total of four nights in space.
  _____

5 If the four-day space trips become popular, the price could reduce eventually.
  _____

6 In 15 years, these kinds of trips might be saw as normal by your children.
  _____

WATCH OUT!

ⓧ Passengers will take
into space by an
experienced crew.

✓ Passengers

_____

into space by an
experienced crew.

C Complete the sentences with the correct form of the words in parentheses. Then write (P) if the action is a possibility or (D) if the action is a definite prediction.

1   Space tourists _____ (*will/give*) a training course. _____
2   The course _____ (*will/hold*) on a tropical island. _____
3   Tourists _____ (*will/not/expect*) to be space experts. _____
4   Critics say the launch date _____ (*might/change*) by the organizers. _____
5   Trips _____ (*may/offer*) by competitors soon. _____
6   If this happens, the price _____ (*could/bring down*). _____
7   Space travel _____ (*may/make*) accessible to everyone in the future. _____
8   Space travel _____ (*will/not/see*) as standard for at least another five years. _____

3 LISTENING: understanding native English speakers

A 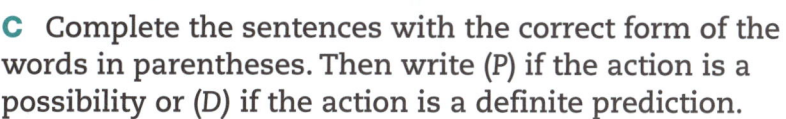 **02 Listen to four people from different places discussing space tourism. Number the places in the order in which you hear them.**

the U.S.A. _____   the U.K. _____   Australia _____   India _____

B Listen again and match the main ideas to the correct speakers. There may be more than one answer for each speaker.

Speaker

a)   there are many ways to enjoy life on Earth   ☐
b)   their lifetime dream will hopefully soon be achieved   ☐
c)   a trip is improbable, but winning the lottery would help ☐
d)   the family watches eclipses and other events from Earth ☐
e)   the price of a space trip is completely impossible to believe ☐
f)   they'll get to see the sun come up many times a day   ☐

A Choose the correct negative prefix for each of the following adjectives.

1	accurate	un-	in-	im-	5	patient	un-	in-	im-
2	believable	un-	in-	im-	6	probable	un-	in-	im-
3	capable	un-	in-	im-	7	significant	un-	in-	im-
4	certain	un-	in-	im-	8	sufficient	un-	in-	im-

B Write each negative adjective from Exercise A next to its definition.

1 not enough _____
2 extraordinary _____
3 disliking waiting _____
4 very small; meaningless _____

5 not sure _____
6 not precise _____
7 not likely to happen _____
8 not able to do something _____

C Complete each sentence with a negative adjective from Exercise A.

1 Scientists are _____ of knowing where an asteroid will land while it's in orbit because they have _____ information.

2 There's a lot of _____ information on the internet about space exploration. If you're _____ whether something is true or not, you should check the fact from a more reliable source.

3 I think it's highly _____ that the Earth will be struck by a huge asteroid. It's sometimes hit by smaller ones, but the damage is usually _____.

4 The station provides the shuttle with a place to go, and the shuttle resupplies the station. It's _____ how we have organized space exploration!

5 Human beings are so _____. They're desperate to understand gravity, the solar system, planets …, but everything will be revealed to us in time.

WATCH OUT!

⊗ Unless you haven't been to space, it is hard to appreciate the beauty of it.

✓ Unless _____ to space, it is hard to appreciate the beauty of it.

A Match the two parts to make complete sentences.

1 Astronauts must not be too tall
2 Journalists can be part of a crew
3 As long as people finance missions,
4 Unless you can cope with zero-gravity,
5 Astronauts learn to fix malfunctions
6 Since much of the work is dangerous,

a) space exploration will continue.
b) you should not even apply for the job!
c) just in case an emergency happens in orbit.
d) since shuttles have limited space.
e) robots are used instead of humans.
f) provided that they receive proper training.

B Choose the correct options to complete the factsheet.

ASTRONAUTS
factsheet

In the 1950s, anyone could apply to be an astronaut **(1)** *since / provided that* they had flight experience and engineering training. In fact, **(2)** *in case / as long as* you had a good educational background, you could apply to be an astronaut without any flying experience. But by 1962, astronauts had no hope of applying **(3)** *as long as / unless* they had excellent academic qualifications, too. Nowadays, candidates have to undergo rigorous physical tests. Their eyes are tested, too, **(4)** *in case / since* they have poor vision. Strict psychological tests are also carried out **(5)** *since / unless* working in the confined space of a shuttle is considered highly stressful. **(6)** *Unless / Provided that* you pass all the tests, you then train for months before joining a mission crew.

6 WRITING: outlining

A Match the notes (A–D) with the correct paragraph heading in the essay outline.

Is it worth undertaking years of training and tests in order to become an astronaut?

Paragraph 1 Introduction: ☐ _____
_____
_____

Paragraph 2 Advantages: ☐ _____
_____

Paragraph 3 Disadvantages: ☐ _____
_____

Paragraph 4 Conclusion: ☐ _____
_____

A Present some of the positive aspects of being an astronaut.

B Children and adults dream of becoming astronauts. Mention why.

C I believe the effort is worth it. Summarize main reason for my opinion.

D Analyze some of the less appealing sides of the job, including training.

B Write 1–4 to explain which paragraph each point belongs to in the essay.

a) A major drawback is the number of years spent undergoing intense training. ☐
b) Despite the rigorous tests and training involved, overall I believe … ☐
c) The opportunity to explore space and float in zero-gravity must be incredible. ☐
d) Ask any young child what they want to be when they grow up … ☐
e) Since a shuttle has limited space, you would be under psychological stress. ☐
f) Provided that you enjoy a challenge, the work would be tremendously exciting. ☐

C Decide if the following are advantages (A), disadvantages (D), or not relevant (NR) in relation to the essay title in Exercise A.

1   You should explore the Earth.   *A / D / NR*
2   You have a chance to contribute to human knowledge.   *A / D / NR*
3   You become one of a small group of people that gets an amazing view of Earth.   *A / D / NR*
4   You spend a lot of time away from home, putting a strain on your family.   *A / D / NR*
5   Gravity has an effect on everybody.   *A / D / NR*
6   It only takes a small medical issue to end your dreams.   *A / D / NR*

skillsStudio

A **Match the words (1–8) to the definitions (a–h).**

1	civilization	**a)**	find suitable people for a job or position
2	colonize	**b)**	put money into, hoping to make a profit
3	estimated	**c)**	make a number or list of things smaller
4	intrepid	**d)**	advanced stage of human social development
5	invest	**e)**	send a group of travelers to a location in order to settle there
6	mundane	**f)**	approximately calculated
7	narrow down	**g)**	adventurous and fearless
8	recruit	**h)**	dull; not exciting

B **03 Listen to a podcast about space exploration. Complete the sentences with a word or short phrase that you hear.**

1 Recruitment is taking place to find people to travel to _____.
2 Selected volunteers will _____ the planet.
3 To be chosen, you need to have an understanding of personal _____ issues.
4 Money for the project will be raised through private _____ and sponsorship.

C Listen again and complete the following sentences with figures from the podcast.

1 It will take _____ days to reach Mars from Earth.
2 There will be _____ people in each shuttle.
3 More than _____ people applied at first.
4 Training for the mission will take _____ years.
5 Just over _____ applicants made it to the round two shortlist.
6 The cost of the project is estimated to be $_____.

D Listen again and choose *T* (true) or *F* (false).

1 The successful recruits will probably return to Earth eventually. *T / F*
2 People applied for the mission from all around the world. *T / F*
3 Heidi Beemer thinks that it's important to be adaptable and resilient. *T / F*
4 Having the right personality is the most important factor in the selection process. *T / F*
5 Heidi Beemer is a recruiting team member for the mission. *T / F*
6 The government will help with some of the funding. *T / F*

E Read the job ad below. Imagine that you want to volunteer as one of the future Mars colonists. Write your application letter, highlighting why you think you would be a perfect person for such a mission. Write 200–220 words.

Mars Inc.—now recruiting!

Position: Mars colonist

We at Mars Inc. are recruiting for an adventurous individual to join our growing space exploration team. The role involves intensive training in preparation for our first expedition to Mars in 2020*.

Please note, we are looking for someone to fit into an existing team, and so personal character is just as important as experience. Full training is provided, but any relevant experience will be beneficial to your application.

Please send a detailed cover letter outlining what you can bring to the team and examples of how you have demonstrated these skills to Mr. R. Manson at Mars Inc.

*Please read the conditions of this expedition carefully before applying.

UNIT 3 PASSWORD PROTECTED

1 READING: text organization

A Read the article. What is the author trying to persuade young people to do?

1 Use social media to show their positive side to employers.
2 Disconnect themselves from social networking sites.
3 Be more careful about what they write online.

 **BigAl95** Really don't wanna go to work. #annoyingboss #lookingforanewjob
1 minute ago   Comment

What your online life can cost you

TECHNOLOGY

1 When Facebook started, it was party pictures and poking—but today it has more far-reaching consequences that young people need to be aware of. Facebook is now one of the first places employers go when they want to find out more about you.

2 We know people have been getting fired for their activity on sites like Twitter, Facebook, and Instagram for a while, but according to a new report, one in 10 young people has been rejected from a job because of the content of their social media profiles.

3 You'd think this widespread rejection would make young people more cautious when posting online, but the report also noted that two-thirds of respondents are not concerned that their social media will damage their careers. That means there's a worrying disconnect between what people think is acceptable to employers online and what's actually acceptable.

4 Even the most relaxed employers tend to have lines in the sand when it comes to what their employees can put online, and many people are facing serious professional repercussions for what they thought were 140 frivolous character tweets and Facebook posts. One woman tweeted that she sometimes wished she could get fired, and the next day she was. That could be you.

5 Sharing work complaints online is never a good idea either. You may think that all of your followers are friends and none of your friends will rat you out, but think again. And there's an internet service, created by the University of Hannover, which gathers the latest tweets showcasing a worker's bad attitude and displays them in a list for all to see. They could easily catch your employer's eye.

6 There is a disconnect between how many people are getting punished for their social media behavior and how confident younger users are that their behavior is appropriate. This means users need to tone it down if they want to keep their professional lives intact. Remember—your boss may not be as cool about those party pictures as you are, and they may get you fired.

Adapted from: www.digitaltrends.com

B Read the article in Exercise A again. Complete the table by summarizing the supporting and concluding points in paragraphs 2–6.

Paragraph	Function
1	Introduction of main point: *Facebook can have a serious impact on your job, as employers use it to find out about you.*
2	Supporting point:
3	Supporting point:
4	Supporting point:
5	Supporting point:
6	Conclusion:

2 VOCABULARY: digital privacy

Choose the correct options to complete the text.

| Home |
| Course information |
| Accommodation |
| University life |
| Safety tips |

In this **(1)** *information age / privacy* where we regularly share news and photos online, it's important that all our students ensure their privacy is not **(2)** *blackmailed / invaded*. Remember that social networks and other companies regularly **(3)** *compile / monitor* their users' online activities. This information may be **(4)** *compiled / monitored* into some kind of **(5)** *database / scam* which could then be sold to other companies. Dishonest companies can try to involve you in their latest **(6)** *blackmail / scam*; you can be a victim of identity **(7)** *scam / theft*; or, more rarely, someone may **(8)** *hack into / blackmail* your computer with the aim of **(9)** *blackmailing / invading* you for money. Avoid **(10)** *compiling / leaving yourself open* to these problems by checking all your social media privacy settings, installing good virus software, and keeping all your passwords private.

3 GRAMMAR: object complements

A Put the words in the correct order. Add commas if necessary.

1 ~~too~~ / personal / us / consider / ~~many~~ / our / secure / information / of
Too many _____

2 ~~when~~ / virus / me / database / helped / Peter / ~~a~~ / recover / my / destroyed / it
When a _____

3 identity / ~~the~~ / described / an / theft / easy / crime / as / ~~man~~
The man _____

4 ~~the~~ / ~~images~~ / thief / security / the / proved / ~~from~~ / she / was / a / camera
The images from _____

WATCH OUT!

(X) She described him an honest man.

(✓) She described him _____ .

B Choose the correct option to complete the sentences.

1 Many celebrities *find it / finds them* frustrating when a reporter takes an unexpected picture.

2 We know these *reporters as / reporters* paparazzi.

3 These pictures sometimes *makes celebrities really angry / make celebrities really angry*.

4 Often, celebrities call reporters *rude / rudeness* for invading their privacy.

5 Personally, I consider *they strange / it strange* because they chose to be famous.

6 I see celebrities *as the main problem / the main problem*.

7 I would *describe them / describe them as* publicity seekers.

8 So, we shouldn't consider *photographers / photographers as* a major threat to privacy.

4 VOCABULARY: phrasal verbs

A Match the phrasal verbs (1–8) with expressions they are commonly used with (a–h).

1	go through	a)	a debt/a phone bill
2	run up	b)	a misunderstanding/a matter
3	call on (someone)	c)	a report/someone's mobile number
4	get out of	d)	to help you/to prove something
5	take out	e)	a bad situation/a difficult time
6	get hold of	f)	doing something different/getting a taxi home
7	clear up	g)	a loan/a mortgage
8	end up	h)	paying a bill/doing the housework

B Complete the story using the correct form of the phrasal verbs from Exercise A.

First Person: Identity Theft

Happened to Me
by Haruki Watanabe

When I first started using a credit card, I didn't consider safety very important but now I know differently. One evening, I went out for dinner with a friend who'd forgotten her wallet, so I **(1)** _____ paying the check. The waiter took my card and went away to process the payment. A month later, I received a bank statement which showed I had **(2)** _____ huge debts. I couldn't believe it! The waiter must have secretly copied my card and then somehow managed to **(3)** _____ my personal details. It took months to **(4)** _____ the matter, especially as the waiter had also **(5)** _____ a couple of loans in my name, but eventually he was arrested. I **(6)** _____ going to court because he pleaded guilty, but I still wouldn't want to **(7)** _____ that again. It was the worst six months of my life. Now I've joined an organization which **(8)** _____ banks to improve their security checks.

5 GRAMMAR: negative structures with *think, suppose*, etc.

A 🎧 04 Listen to each conversation. Choose the missing response.

1	a) ☐ I believe so.			4	a) ☐ I imagine so.	
	b) ☐ I suppose not.				b) ☐ I don't suppose so.	
2	a) ☐ I imagine so.			5	a) ☐ I suspect so.	
	b) ☐ I hope not.				b) ☐ I guess not.	
3	a) ☐ I think so.			6	a) ☐ I hope so.	
	b) ☐ I don't believe so.				b) ☐ I don't think so.	

B Read the online conversation. Write sentences with negative structures using the prompts in parentheses.

Earlier messages: 1 day   1 week   2 week   1 month   3 months   6 months   1 year   All

Durak says:
Do your teenage kids spend a lot of time alone in their rooms?

Mo says:
All the time! **(1)** _____ (*I/imagine/there's/anything*) I can do about it, though.

Durak says:
No, **(2)** _____ (*I/guess*). **(3)** _____ (*I/suppose/the kids/want/it*) to change.

Mo says:
Probably not! Our doctor said teenagers need their privacy.
He said **(4)** _____ (*they/feel/they/have/anything*) in common with us anymore, just their peers.

Durak says:
Well, **(5)** _____ (*I/hope/I/have/anything*) in common with my son's peers. **(6)** _____ (*I/think/I/understand*) a single word they say, and the music they listen to is awful.

Mo says:
Well, I think that's normal. No doubt our parents said the same about our friends!

> **WATCH OUT!**
> ✗ I don't suppose they aren't interested.
> ✓ I don't suppose _____ .

---

6 COMMUNICATION STRATEGY: participating in a group discussion

A Draw lines to match the two parts to make complete sentences.

1 ☐ Why don't we start by
2 ☐ Who wants
3 ☐ Sorry to stop you, but maybe
4 ☐ I don't mean to interrupt you,
5 ☐ The next point for discussion is
6 ☐ I don't think we've heard
7 ☐ Maybe we should move on
8 ☐ So, does anyone else want to add anything
9 ☐ I apologize for interrupting, but

a) to discussing whether this loss of privacy is a problem…
b) … but can you speak up a little?
c) anything from you on the subject.
d) discussing what we all learnt about privacy…?
e) before we start writing…?
f) we should focus on the topic at hand.
g) haven't we just talked about that?
h) to start?
i) whether privacy is a luxury.

B Match each sentence (1–9) from Exercise A with its use.

a) Interrupting politely ___ ___ ___
b) Starting, finishing, or keeping the discussion moving ___ ___ ___
c) Inviting contributions ___ ___ ___

C 🎧 05 Listen to three extracts from a group discussion and check the sentences from Exercise A that you hear.

A **Read the article. Choose the correct option to answer to the questions.**

1 Where do individuals feel more strongly about the right to privacy? *the U.S.A. / Europe*
2 Where are data protection laws stricter? *the U.S.A. / Europe*
3 Where is the punishment for breaking data laws stricter? *the U.S.A. / Europe*

B **Complete the collocations (1–7) with words from the article. Match each collocation to its definition (a–f). One definition can be used twice.**

1 data _____
2 fundamental _____
3 private _____
4 sensitive _____
5 strict _____
6 tax _____
7 zip _____

a) an agreement which must be obeyed completely
b) legal control over who can see or use information held on computers
c) information that needs to be kept secret or dealt with carefully
d) a group of numbers that you add to the end of a person's address
e) documents which hold information about money you pay to the government
f) an essential thing you are allowed to have by law

C **Match a heading to each paragraph. Three headings are not needed.**

Paragraph 1
Paragraph 2
Paragraph 3
Paragraph 4
Paragraph 5
Paragraph 6
Paragraph 7
Paragraph 8

a) Restrictions for retailers
b) Getting hold of sensitive information
c) Less opposition to sharing information
d) An increasing loss of control
e) A case of two perspectives
f) Lack of serious consequences for some
g) Governments refusing to play by the rules
h) Happy to pay for personal data
i) Passing on data without question
j) Strict regulations
k) Contrasting legal systems

D **Read the following essay prompt. Write an essay of at least 250 words.**

Some people say that the ability to ask for your personal data to be deleted is an important human right. Others suggest it is impossible to enforce. Discuss both these views and give your own opinion.

ACCESS DENIED

Playing it safe or playing it cool?

Differing attitudes toward privacy in the U.S.A. and Europe

[1] Given the many economic, cultural, and social similarities between Europe and the U.S.A., it may come as a surprise to learn that there is a very large difference between these two places when it comes to the question of personal data protection. In the U.S.A., privacy is simply an economic and consumer issue; for Europeans, it is considered a fundamental right that should be protected and supported by law.

[2] In Europe, data protection is controlled by a set of principles that both businesses and the government are required to comply with. Businesses are prevented from buying and selling personal information without the consent of the individual. European citizens tend to be automatically suspicious of giving out personal information and will often want to know why it is being requested and how it will be used.

[3] In contrast, Americans are much less likely to complain about companies handling their personal data although they are mistrustful of it ending up in the government's hands. Data such as tax records and mortgage information are widely available to the public, and businesses are free to collect and sell information about their customers as they wish. If there are ever any debates over data protection, these tend to relate to government or individual cases where privacy laws have been broken by businesses.

[4] If you go into stores in the U.S.A. and Europe, the effect of these differences is apparent. In some European countries, certain data such as zip codes and phone numbers can only be requested if the customer is paying by card, and even then the information can only be kept if there is a specific reason to do so. Other European countries require employees who handle personal and very sensitive data to sign a strict agreement preventing them from forwarding it on to other organizations.

[5] Yet in the U.S.A., customers seem relaxed about giving up their personal information in stores and are willing to hand over information that Europeans would refuse access to. They rarely ask why it is being collected or what will happen to their data as a result. American companies keep personal data as a matter of course and routinely make money selling it on to third party organizations who can then sell their own products or services directly to those customers.

[6] The regulations which cover both the U.S.A. and Europe operate differently too. In the U.S.A., there is a patchwork of laws which differ across states.

What is law in one state may not be law in another, and in some cases, may actually contradict the law elsewhere. To make things more complex, the government also provides guidelines for companies to work within. These guidelines are not enforceable by law but they are considered to be examples of best practice that companies should follow. On the other hand, in Europe, the E.U. is bringing in regulations to unify laws across member countries so a company in one country will be required to deal with data in exactly the same way in all E.U. countries. The regulations will also see more power given to the individual who will be able to request to see any information held about them and ask for it to be deleted if they wish—the so-called "Right to be forgotten" principle.

[7] It is interesting to note, however, that despite the stricter laws, if companies in Europe do break these rules, they are unlikely to be punished severely. Indeed, it appears as if regulators are almost unable to enforce these laws despite the importance placed on them. Businesses that are too free and easy with their customers' data tend to be dealt with informally, rather than taken to court and fined. In contrast, in the U.S.A., firms are expected to self-regulate, but when they fail to do so, the Federal Trade Commission (FTC) is only too happy to step in and fight unfair practices in court.

[8] So it seems that Europe and the U.S.A. operate in different ways when it comes to data protection, both culturally and legally. But in both parts of the world, it is becoming more and more difficult to control what is being kept private and what our private information is being used for. Therefore we can expect to see continued changes as both the U.S.A. and Europe attempt to keep up with our ever-changing, technological world.

UNIT 4   A NEW LOOK AT LEARNING

1 VOCABULARY: verb collocations

A Match each verb or phrase (1–6) with a list of typical collocations (a–f).

1   drop out of
2   set
3   be faced with
4   take into
5   get
6   offer a broad range of

a) choices/courses/alternatives
b) account/consideration
c) a class/a group/college
d) a college degree/into debt/a chance/a taste/a college education
e) problems/distractions/peer pressure
f) goals/a date/a time/a schedule

B Complete the ad with the correct form of the phrases from Exercise A.

Axford College

"When I **(1)** _____ college for the second time, my parents were furious. I don't blame them. After all, they **(2)** _____ the problem of paying my tuition fees. But I thought I had ruined my chances forever of **(3)** _____ a college degree until I discovered online learning with Axford College. And it really works for me! Now I **(4)** _____ my own goals and I **(5)** _____ not _____ the distractions I had on campus—or large tuition fees! Axford College **(6)** _____ online classes, so there are options for everyone. The classes **(7)** _____ our different learning styles _____ account, so that they work for you! And we **(8)** _____ the chance to talk to a tutor once a week. So, if on-campus college is not for you, try online learning with Axford College. It's great!"

2 GRAMMAR: relative pronouns with *–ever*

A Complete the sentences with the correct relative pronoun: *whatever, whenever, however, whoever,* or *wherever.*

1   You can use this app to help you study _____ you are—even in the bathroom!
2   Sarah always finishes at the top of the class, _____ test she takes.
3   _____ wants to take this class is welcome—just register online.
4   _____ you want to study is up to you. For example, working alone, in groups, online—anything is OK.
5   You can call me _____ you like—I'll always be happy to help.

WATCH OUT!

✗ Whatever you cook for dinner, I'm sure they will be delicious.

✓ Whatever you cook for dinner, I'm sure _____ delicious.

B Read the email on page 23 and underline the four relative pronoun mistakes. Write the correct sentences below.

1   _____
2   _____
3   _____
4   _____

To: c.broudy@macmillan.ac ✕   Send ✉

Dear Professor Broudy,

I hope you don't mind me writing to you. My name is Pascale Dubois, and I took your film studies class last semester. I enjoyed it very much! Whatever we studied topic, you always stimulated the class. So, I'd really like to take your class again, but I have some questions.

This coming semester, I see that you're teaching Advanced Film Studies, but it's an online class. So, does that mean we can view each week's material whoever we want, or is there an assigned meeting time for viewing? Also, I noticed that there are four essays we need to submit across the semester. Do we have to submit online, or can we submit whenever we want (for example, giving to you in person, leaving in your mailbox, and so on)? Finally, whoever wants to join the class are able to—is that correct? I'm asking because my friend is actually an economics major, but he's heard really good things about your class and he wants to take it too.

3 LISTENING: understanding non-native English speakers

A 🎧 **06** Listen to three speakers. One is from Brazil, one from the United Arab Emirates, and one from Germany. Listen carefully to their accents and decide where each speaker is from.

1 **a)** Brazil   **b)** United Arab Emirates   **c)** Germany
2 **a)** Brazil   **b)** United Arab Emirates   **c)** Germany
3 **a)** Brazil   **b)** United Arab Emirates   **c)** Germany

B Listen again and choose the correct option a, b, or c.

1 According to speaker 1, why do more people prefer subjects like media studies these days?
   a) They are easier.
   b) They are more interesting.
   c) They are more practical.

2 What does speaker 1 think about more people doing internships?
   a) It's a great idea.
   b) It's a bad idea.
   c) Not sure if it's a good idea or not.

3 According to speaker 2, who are the online courses mostly aimed at?
   a) People in urban areas.
   b) People in rural areas.
   c) People with cell phones.

4 Why does speaker 2 think many people drop out of online courses?
   a) They feel separated from other people.
   b) They don't discipline themselves.
   c) They don't like living in rural areas.

5 How does speaker 3 describe the equipment at the universities?
   a) It's very old.
   b) It's of bad quality.
   c) It's very modern.

6 According to speaker 3, which of the following is true?
   a) Students from far away cannot stay at the campus.
   b) The culture and customs of other countries are given priority.
   c) The teaching has an international outlook.

4 GRAMMAR: mixed conditionals

A **Choose the correct meaning of each sentence.**

1 If I had better IT skills, I probably would have gotten a better job.
   a) I have good IT skills, but I didn't get a very good job.
   b) I didn't get a very good job because I don't have good IT skills.

2 I would be unemployed now if I hadn't studied IT.
   a) I have a job now because I studied IT.
   b) I don't have a job now because I didn't study IT.

B **Complete the sentences using *would*, *wouldn't*, *had*, or *hadn't*.**

1 If you _____ taken this job, where would you be working now?

2 If we had studied harder in college, we _____ have well-paid jobs now.

3 My English would be better if my teacher _____ used a better methodology.

4 If I had studied statistics, I _____ need to take a course in it now.

5 I think I _____ have better managerial skills if I'd chosen business studies.

6 If we _____ missed so many computer programming classes, we would know how to code this software.

> **WATCH OUT!**
>
> ✗ If I would have paid more attention in IT, I would know more now.
>
> ✓ _____ more attention in IT, I would know more now.

C **Read the conversation below. Complete the sentences using mixed conditionals and the verbs in parentheses.**

Zara: Did you read that article about overseas students? It says they used to like studying in the U.K., but now they prefer the U.S.A. because there's a friendlier study environment here!

Lucho: I can believe that. But we haven't invested enough in state-of-the-art equipment. Many overseas students prefer Australia now because it has invested in facilities.

Zara: That's too bad. We've lost a lot of overseas students because of that lack of investment. I think we overcharge, too, and that's another reason fewer students come from abroad. A lot of students are looking for more reasonably-priced courses. I heard South East Asia is seeing an increase in this area.

Lucho: Right! And we haven't done enough to advertise. Other places have made more of an effort to promote themselves, and that's helped them attract a lot more students. We should do the same, and perhaps then more students would want to stay here.

1 If the U.K. had had a friendlier study environment, more overseas students _____ (choose) to study there.

2 Australia wouldn't attract so many overseas students if it _____ (invest) in facilities.

3 If the U.S.A. didn't overcharge, it _____ (lose) a lot of overseas students.

4 If other places _____ (promote) themselves, they wouldn't be so popular now.

5 If the U.S.A. promoted itself more, more overseas students _____ (stay).

6 If the U.S.A. had invested in better equipment, more overseas students _____ (prefer) to study there.

5 VOCABULARY: words related to *stand*

Complete the sentences with the correct form of the words and phrases from the box.

> it stands to reason   outstanding   stand a chance   stand back
> stand out   standard   standing   where something/someone stands

1 A degree from a college of high _____ used to guarantee you a good job—but not anymore!
2 People who drop out of high school don't _____ of getting into a top college.
3 _____ that if you skip a lot of classes and don't do the assignments, your GPA will be very low.
4 From _____ I'm _____, you deserve to be very successful—I've watched you work really hard for many years!
5 Nowadays, _____ in hiring have changed. Employers want more.
6 Candidates _____ more if they have writing and management skills.
7 The best, or most _____ candidates, are those with "soft skills."
8 I can't believe that. You saw him cheat on the test and you just _____ and did nothing.

6 WRITING: sentence variety — punctuation with connectors

A Read the public's comments in response to an online article about falling educational standards. Underline two connectors in each post.

| WORLD | BUSINESS | TECHNOLOGY | SCIENCE | SPORTS | ARTS | LIFESTYLE | OPINION |

Failing standards, failing nation *by Dave Lemont*
Read article   Readers' comments
R. Shaw, Boston, 9:30 a.m.
1 Because the young are more interested in the life of reality show celebrities and other so-called stars they don't care about important issues anymore. In addition, their parents don't care!
jimmyt, Adelaide, 10:07 a.m.
2 @R. Shaw: I kind of agree with you, however, has it occurred to you that the fault lies with the media itself, not with the young or the parents? Also, I found a punctuation mistake in your comment. Before you criticize young people's standards raise your own!
3 tc1999, Osaka, 9:41a.m.
Although you're right to say students could help themselves more, it's unfair to blame them since the cost of getting a degree is huge. If it hadn't become so expensive, more people would study.
4 mariemarie, Nice, 11:44 a.m.
It is often said that today's young are tomorrow's leaders. Therefore it stands to reason that today's parents are the parents of tomorrow's leaders. You blame the young but maybe you should stand back from the situation and take a good look at today's parents!

B Find six punctuation mistakes in Exercise A. Rewrite each sentence with the correct punctuation.

1 _____
2 _____
3 _____
4 _____
5 _____
6 _____

skillsStudio

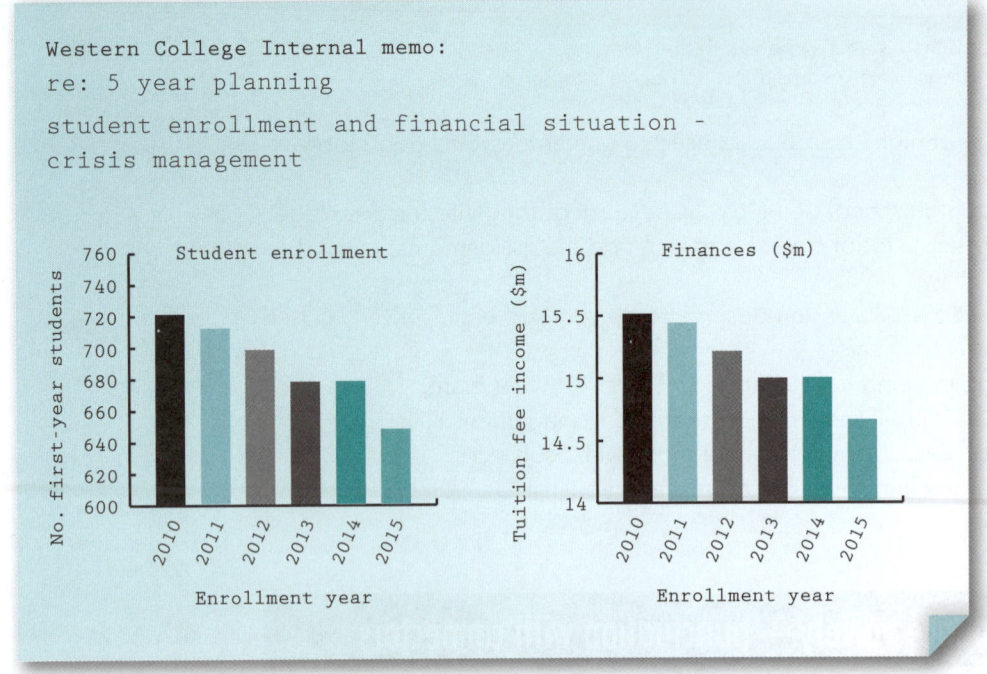

Western College Internal memo:
re: 5 year planning

student enrollment and financial situation -
crisis management

A Look at the charts above. Answer the questions.

1 What is the difference between the number of first-year students in 2010 and 2013 at Western College?
   a) 40 more students in 2013
   b) 40 fewer students in 2013
   c) 50 more students in 2013
   d) 50 fewer students in 2013

2 What is the best way to describe the finances of Western College?
   a) healthy
   b) growing
   c) declining
   d) bankrupt

3 What word best predicts the future for Western College?
   a) declining
   b) improving
   c) cautious
   d) outstanding

B Match the words and phrases (1–7) to the definitions (a–g).

1 curriculum
2 decline
3 potential
4 quota
5 revenue
6 subsidy
7 tuition fees

a) to become less or worse
b) income from business activities
c) an amount of something that someone is officially allowed to have
d) an amount of money that the government pays to help reduce the cost of a product or service
e) possible or likely in the future
f) money that you pay to take classes, especially at a college, university, or private school
g) the subjects that students study at a particular school or college

C 🎧 **07** **Listen to a professor give a talk to her colleagues. Answer the questions.**

1 How does the professor describe the Western College's reputation?
   a) terrible
   b) bad
   c) average
   d) good
2 How is Western College's equipment described?
   a) old-fashioned
   b) modern
   c) expensive
   d) cheap
3 What does DE stand for?
   a) distance e-learning
   b) deeper e-learning
   c) distance education
   d) deeper education
4 What does the professor not mention as a benefit of DE?
   a) It's less expensive.
   b) There's more flexibility.
   c) There's no inconvenience of commuting to campus.
   d) It's easier to generate academic discussions online.
5 What is the professor's conclusion?
   a) It's too late to start DE.
   b) It's not too late to start DE.
   c) Western College should not have adapted sooner.
   d) Western College should wait before moving to DE.

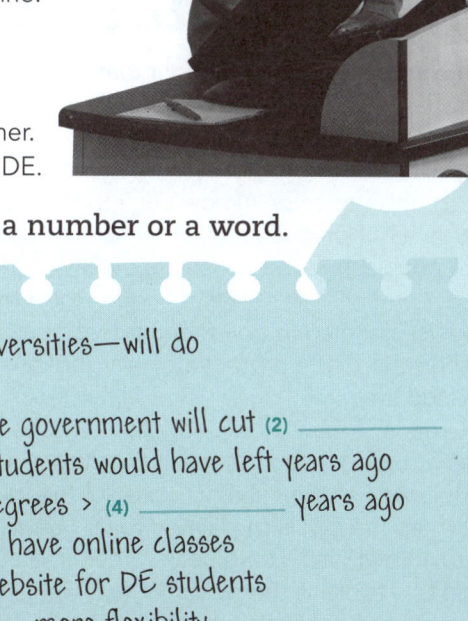

D **Listen again and complete the notes with a number or a word.**

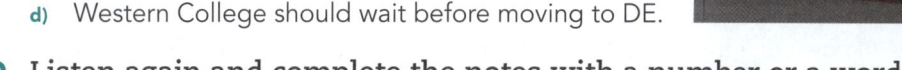

Government wants to reduce # of colleges & universities—will do this over the next (1) _____ years
If college doesn't meet quota 5 years in a row, the government will cut (2) _____
Education not poor (3) _____—otherwise students would have left years ago
University of London started distance learning degrees > (4) _____ years ago
(5) _____% of colleges and universities now have online classes
(6) _____% of community colleges have a website for DE students
(7) _____% of students think online classes = more flexibility
Since 2000, market for online classes grown by (8) _____%

E **Would you prefer to take a traditional classroom-based course or a distance education course? Write an essay outlining which you would prefer and why. Write 200–260 words.**

UNIT 5 ON THE WILD SIDE

1 GRAMMAR: impersonal passive

A Complete the second sentence so it means the same as the first.
Write no more than four words.

1 Experts believe that there are over 200 species of owl in the world.
It _____ there are over 200 species of owl in the world.

2 Some people report that the owl population of some species is lower than in the past.
The owl population of some species _____ lower than in the past.

3 Experts understand that owls can turn their head up to 270°.
It _____ owls can turn their heads up to 270°.

4 People assume that owls make just one sound—a hoot.
Owls _____ just one sound—a hoot.

5 In fact, experts say that owls make a variety of different sounds.
Owls _____ a variety of different sounds.

6 Experts know some species of owl eat fish as well as mammals.
It _____ some species of owl eat fish as well as mammals.

> ### WATCH OUT!
>
> ✗ Owls think to be unlucky in some cultures.
> ✓ Owls _____ to be unlucky in some cultures.

B Choose the correct options to complete the article.

species | facts | pictures

Myths and Culture

Owls are **(1)** *considered to be* / *thought that* both good and evil in cultures around the world. They are birds which silently prey on small mammals at night with incredible skill and intelligence. It is **(2)** *understood to be* / *thought that* these attributes contribute to both the positive and negative image of an owl.

Owls were **(3)** *believed to be* / *known that* the protector of the dead in Ancient Egypt and a predictor of death in Ancient Rome. Depictions of the Aztec God of Death would often feature an owl. Still today, some people in Kenya associate owls with death, and among some Native American tribes, a dream about an owl is **(4)** *said that* / *understood to* predict death or illness.

Owls are not **(5)** *assumed to be* / *thought that* a bad omen by all Native American tribes, however. Some describe them as a protector of warriors or suggest they are the souls of people who have recently passed away.

In Ancient Greece, Athena, the Goddess of Wisdom, chose the owl to be her protector, and this association with wisdom continues in the West today. In Japan, it is **(6)** *reported to be* / *said that* owls bring good luck due to their ability to predict the weather.

Among the Inuit, the owl is **(7)** *claimed to be* / *understood that* a young girl who was magically changed into an owl with a long beak. When she became frightened, she hit the side of a building, and this explains the owl's flat face and short beak today.

Whatever a culture's belief about the owl, **(8)** *it can certainly be said* / *they can certainly be thought* that it is an animal with a strong identity.

2 VOCABULARY: animal rescue

A 🎧 08 Listen and write the words and phrases you hear.

1 _____   4 _____
2 _____   5 _____
3 _____   6 _____

B Complete the text with the words and phrases from Exercise A.

| HOME | ANIMALS | FACTS | CONSERVATION WORK | ENVIRONMENT |

White Rhino

The **(1)** _____ of the northern white rhino is in Central Africa. This rhino is now extinct in the **(2)** _____, so the seven remaining rhinos live in zoos or conservation parks. To increase the numbers of this seriously **(3)** _____, an attempt is being made to breed it **(4)** _____. There is no chance of **(5)** _____ for the newborns, because they are either shot by poachers or sold to **(6)** _____.

3 GRAMMAR: passive modals

A Decide if the passive modals in bold refer to the present (Pr), the future (F), or the past (Pa).

1 _____ Conservation parks **should be** better **funded**.
2 _____ Animals conservation laws **may be changed**.
3 _____ Some extinct species **might have been saved** if we had acted sooner.
4 _____ There **can't** only **be** a handful of northern rhinos **left**. There must be more.
5 _____ The habitat of some species has almost disappeared. It **should have been protected**.
6 _____ Illegal hunting **must be eliminated**.

B Choose the correct options to complete the conversation.

Dan: Why are northern white rhinos being kept in conservation parks or zoos? They shouldn't have **(1)** *taken away* / *been taken away* from their natural habitat.

Sue: Because they were almost extinct in Central Africa, that's why.

Dan: Well, people ought to have **(2)** *protected* / *been protected* them better. They can't have **(3)** *looked after* / *been looked after* the animals very well.

Sue: I guess poachers are to blame. They're the ones hunting these animals to make money.

Dan: Well, at least the newborns can **(4)** *released* / *be released* into the wild. They shouldn't **(5)** *brought up* / *be brought up* in captivity.

Sue: I'm sure the conservationists will **(6)** *set them free* / *be set them free* one day. But first a safe place should **(7)** *found* / *be found* for them. Preferably somewhere where they might **(8)** *given* / *be given* the chance to repopulate.

WATCH OUT!

✗ The elephants ought to have released into the wild.

✓ The elephants ought to _____ into the wild.

4 COMMUNICATION STRATEGY: summarizing

A Read the forum post. Identify the writer's point of view about wild animals in city limits and the four reasons given. Write a summary of these in your own words.

HOME   NEWS   SPORT   WEATHER   EDITOR'S COMMENT

East Coast
Daily

Thursday, November 10 2:56   5 Comments

Wild animals: their home, too

The wild animals recently seen in New York should not have been shot, especially the female white-tailed deer. I think that animals should be allowed inside the city limits. After all, they were in the city long before us! In the case of the coyotes sighted in Central Park, it seems somewhat hypocritical of us to assume that we humans can use their habitats (think of the national parks we destroy!), but they can't use our habitat. Anyway, doesn't wildlife make the city a more attractive place? Personally, I'd like to see lots of deer in East Harlem. As for the harbor seals seen off Staten Island, they are a previously endangered species. And now they're back in large numbers. So let's be happy that our conservation efforts have worked. Also, their return is proof that our waterways are cleaner at last. So surely the animals should be welcomed back.

The editor of the East Coast Daily believes that _____
_____
_____
_____
_____
_____

B 🎧 09 Listen to the summary. Compare it with your summary from Exercise A.

5 VOCABULARY: adverb-adjective collocations

A Cross out the adverb that cannot be used with each adjective in bold.

	a)		b)		c)		
1	a)	highly	b)	over	c)	under	**estimated**
2	a)	poorly	b)	badly	c)	under	**organized**
3	a)	well	b)	poorly	c)	highly	**done**
4	a)	poorly	b)	under	c)	over	**populated**

B Complete the sentences with different adverbs from Exercise A.

1 National parks are _____ utilized. Why don't more people visit them?
2 We need a _____ thought-out plan to keep coyotes out of cities.
3 The city is _____ populated with rats. They are everywhere!
4 The publicity campaign was _____ done. No one understood it.
5 Bears should be kept out of our cities. They are _____ dangerous.

6 READING: understanding definitions

A Read the article. Choose *T* (true) or *F* (false) for each statement.

1 The article is about the decline in the quality of life for animals.   *T / F*
2 The problem is largely caused by human beings.   *T / F*
3 People are at last beginning to pay attention to the dangers.   *T / F*

| SEARCH |

HOME   NEWS   GLOBAL ISSUES   DONATING   OUR WORK   VOLUNTEERING   CONTACT US

CONSERVATION WORLDWIDE

One in Four Mammals Face Extinction

[1]Conservationists are shocked by the extent of animal decline. [2]According to a list compiled by the IUCN, or International Union for Conservation of Nature, a total of 19,817 species are facing extinction. [3]This figure is up from 16,306 in 2008.

[4]The IUCN predicts that nearly a quarter of mammal species, including the Iberian lynx and the western gorilla, could be lost completely within our lifetime.

[5]The Tasmanian Devil—a kind of large marsupial—might also disappear.

[6]Julia Marton-Lefevre, Chief of the IUCN, said that these species will be "lost as a result of our own actions," that is, killed off by human activities such as hunting.

[7]One mammal affected by irresponsible human actions is the Fishing Cat—a kind of wild cat—which has become highly endangered due to the draining of land, pollution, and over-fishing. [8]Another seriously threatened species is the Sumatran Orangutan, which is losing its natural habitat to make way for palm oil plantations, an action known as habitat conversion.

[9]Dr. Mark Wright, of the WWFUK (which is the UK branch of the World Wildlife Fund Network) said, "The report shows that, with our ill-considered management of the Earth and its resources, we are threatening the future of wildlife and nature and denying our children the chance to experience what we have experienced."

[10]Dr. Wright also points out that the public is getting too used to seeing negative reports about the decline of animals. [11]He worries that we have become "deadened."

[12]That is, we hear so much bad news, we don't pay attention anymore.

[13]Indeed, little mention is made of the success stories.

[14]Some mammal species, including the African elephant and the black-footed ferret, are recovering after dropping to record lows. [15]And the wild horse, extinct in the wild a decade ago, now totals 325 in Mongolia, where it was re-introduced. [16]Proof that it's not all bad news out there.

Adapted from www.mirror.co.uk

B Read the article in Exercise A again. Identify the nine sentences which include a definition.

— — — — — — — —

skillsStudio

A Read the article on the opposite page. Answer the questions.

1 Which animal population is the highest? _____
2 Which animal has the largest number of species? _____
3 Which animal has experienced the highest loss of numbers? _____

B Read the article again. Complete each sentence with one word from the text.

1 Apes have provided us with _____ into the life of early man.
2 Primates _____ the remains of fruit they eat across the forest floor.
3 A bat is a _____ of insects and can catch them in mid-air.
4 Bats are important for our ecosystem because of their _____.
5 Plants need bees to breed following thousands of centuries of _____.
6 Plankton describes _____ and very small creatures.

C In which fact file are the following mentioned? Choose from fact files A, B, C, or D in the text.

1 They help keep down the population of small winged animals. __
2 These animals make up one fifth of all mammals. __
3 They are important for our atmosphere. __ __
4 Without them, certain plants will not survive. __ __
5 They are financially significant. __ __
6 They make up the largest group of mammals on the planet. __
7 They are involved in the growing of new plants. __ __ __
8 They stop the ground from being damaged. __
9 They would have a large effect on food supply if they became extinct. __
10 They can find the precise location of another animal. __
11 They have been affected by a medical condition. __
12 There is a common misconception about them. __
13 The biology of these animals amazed experts. __
14 These animals are negatively affected by plant chemicals. __
15 A fifth of total species are in danger. __

D Read the job advertisement. Write a letter of application between 220 and 260 words.

We are inviting applications for part-time work at our *Bringing Back the Bee* organization. We work with the local community and government and aim to increase bee numbers in the area by 25% over the next three years. If you would like to help us meet our aim, then please answer the following questions:

1. Why are you interested in our project?
2. What skills can you bring to our project?
3. What relevant work experience do you have?

Mrs. L Rose

Bringing Back the Bee

The animals
we can't live without

We are all aware of the thousands of animal species threatened with extinction and our need to maintain biodiversity in order for our planet to continue. But which animals are the most important to human life? Here are fact files about four animals we cannot live without.

A There are 400,000 great apes and a billion other primates. Of the 394 different species, 114 of them are threatened with extinction, with bush meat hunters and habitat loss as the main threats. Primates share more than 90 % of our DNA, with the similarities between a chimpanzee's genetic code and our own code surprising even the experts. By studying monkeys and apes, we have been able to gain a remarkable insight into our own beginnings and into how our complex cultures have developed.

Primates are also of great economic importance in many countries. In Rwanda and Uganda, for example, the Mountain gorillas are now the number one source of foreign currency income through tourism. Perhaps more importantly, primates disperse seeds around the forest as they eat fruits. "Primates are a keystone species in tropical rainforests. We need to protect primates today in order to have forests tomorrow that can absorb carbon dioxide and prevent the erosion of soil," says Ian Redmond, chairperson for Ape Alliance, an international coalition of organizations and individuals working for the conservation and welfare of apes.

B Bats are the most abundant mammal on the planet—one in five mammals is a bat. There are 1,100 species; however, one in every five of them is threatened from both habitat loss and their reputation for being blood suckers, even though most feed on insects and fruit. Bats are the only mammal capable of flying and are so highly evolved, they can identify the position of a single insect flying in the dark and pull it directly out of the air. For this reason, they are a major predator of insects and play a key role in controlling insect numbers.

That is not the only benefit they offer, however. "Bats have an extraordinary diversity, which makes them an essential part of the ecosystem," says Dr. Kate Jones, a bat expert from the Zoological Society of London. "They are also a key indicator species that can provide information on the health of an ecosystem. They occupy a wide range of habitats, from urban areas to caves and forests. Most crucially, bats are major agents of pollination and seed dispersal. Without them, many crops would fail because they play such an essential part of the ecosystem."

C There are 20,000 known species of bee and billions of individuals, with a single bee hive containing up to 40,000 bees. However, disease and climate change have seen populations fall by up to 80%. Unfortunately, without bees, humans would starve.

These hard-working little insects are the world's greatest pollinators, carrying pollen from flower to flower. Millions of years of evolution have seen many plants rely almost completely upon bees to help them breed. Crops such as almonds, peaches, avocados, and apricots rely solely on bee pollination. The total worldwide economic value of pollination has been estimated to be around $200 billion a year, and that is without the honey and wax that bees also produce. George McGavin, from Oxford University's Museum of Natural History, says, "The planet could go on functioning quite happily without any large animals such as primates. We rely upon bees for just about every vegetable, flower, and fruit around. We would face mass starvation without them."

D Plankton, that is anything living in water that is too small to swim against the ocean current, is hard to love. However, there are 50,000 different species of plankton in the light zone of the ocean alone and billions of trillions of plankton exist. This floating soup of tiny creatures and bacteria can be seen from space and can help billions of marine creatures to live. And yet it is threatened by pesticides and pollution.

The plant-like organisms in plankton, known as phytoplankton, are found close to the surface of the water where there is sufficient light to allow photosynthesis. "Half of the world's oxygen is produced by these organisms," explains Professor David Thomas, from the University of Bangor. "If you took that away, you would lose the basis of life on the globe. There simply wouldn't be enough oxygen to support life." The bacteria also provide a vital role by breaking down organic material in the water and recycling dead organisms.

Adapted from www.telegraph.co.uk

UNIT 6   MORE THAN MACHINES?

1 GRAMMAR: future perfect

A Choose the correct option to complete the sentences.

1 In 20 years, machines *will have taken over* / *will have been taken over by* many jobs that humans do now.

2 By the year 2025, humans *won't have replaced* / *will have been replaced by* robots in factories.

3 The lives of people with disabilities *will have improved* / *will have been improved by* robots in 10 years.

4 Fifteen years from now, people still *won't have invented* / *won't have been invented by* robots with feelings.

5 Microsurgery *will have significantly enhanced* / *will have been significantly enhanced by* technological innovation.

6 By 2040, we *will have developed* / *will have been developed by* machines to do most household tasks.

B Complete the forum post. Use the future perfect form of the verbs in parentheses.

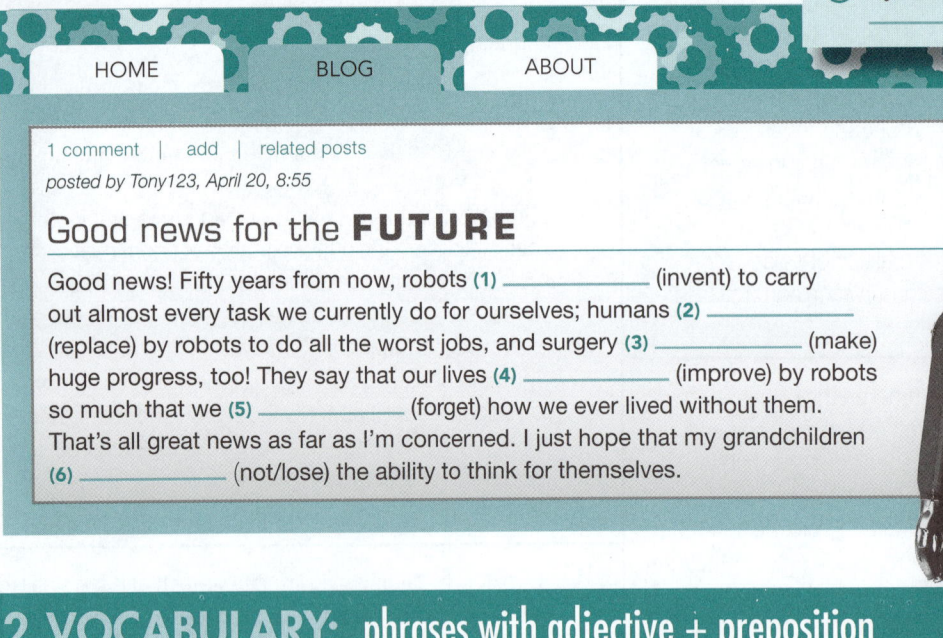

HOME | BLOG | ABOUT

1 comment | add | related posts
posted by Tony123, April 20, 8:55

Good news for the **FUTURE**

Good news! Fifty years from now, robots **(1)** _____ (invent) to carry out almost every task we currently do for ourselves; humans **(2)** _____ (replace) by robots to do all the worst jobs, and surgery **(3)** _____ (make) huge progress, too! They say that our lives **(4)** _____ (improve) by robots so much that we **(5)** _____ (forget) how we ever lived without them. That's all great news as far as I'm concerned. I just hope that my grandchildren **(6)** _____ (not/lose) the ability to think for themselves.

> ### WATCH OUT!
>
> ✗ By the time I graduate, my IT skills will become obsolete.
>
> ✓ By the time I graduate, my IT skills _____ obsolete.

2 VOCABULARY: phrases with adjective + preposition

A Complete the expressions with the prepositions *by*, *of*, or *on*.

1 be alarmed _____
2 be overwhelmed _____
3 be focused _____
4 be suspicious _____
5 be dependent _____
6 be aware _____
7 be distracted _____

B Match the phrases from Exercise A (1–7) to their definitions (a–g).

a) be unable to concentrate on something ___
b) need or rely on someone or something ___
c) concentrate on a particular aim ___
d) be frightened or worried ___
e) know about a situation or fact ___
f) feel that someone or something cannot be trusted ___
g) be unable to deal with a large amount of something ___

C Complete the sentences with the correct form of the expressions from Exercise A.

1 In the future, perhaps humans will be too _____ machines.
2 Most people _____ not _____ how their lives are already mechanized.
3 How can you work with music playing? _____ you not _____ it?
4 I _____ scientists' claims. I mean, we have no idea if they're true.
5 Doctors _____ the number of accidents caused by machines that have been reported in the news.
6 It's hard to _____ my work with all these noisy machines around.
7 I _____ so _____ all this work—I'm not sure how I'll get it done in time.

3 LISTENING: inferring opinions

A 》📻10 **Listen to the conversation. Choose the correct option to answer the questions.**

1 According to Kate, what will the robots of the future be like?
  a) rigid
  b) flexible
  c) glossy
  d) metallic
2 How do the robots change shape?
  a) the same as normal robots
  b) by squeezing into a small space
  c) by adding or removing air
  d) by changing their material
3 According to Kate, which statement is false?
  a) The robots will help to cut open humans for surgery.
  b) The robots could travel inside humans.
  c) The movement of the robots is based on some animals.
  d) The robots might perform delicate medical operations in the future.

B Listen again and check the best paraphrase of the sentences. Consider use of emphasis, word choice, and tone of voice to help infer the speaker's meaning.

1 Mark: I guess, yeah. _____
  ☐ Absolutely!   ☐ Not really.
2 Mark: They are? _____
  ☐ I didn't know that.   ☐ Did you know that?
3 Mark: Whatever you say. _____
  ☐ I don't agree with you.   ☐ I agree with you.
4 Mark: And pigs might fly! _____
  ☐ Science is amazing.   ☐ That will never happen.
5 Kate: Fine! _____
  ☐ That's not OK.   ☐ That's OK.

C Listen again and note which of the following helped you to understand the meaning. Write the correct letter(s) next to the sentences in Exercise B.

a) use of emphasis   b) word choice   c) tone of voice

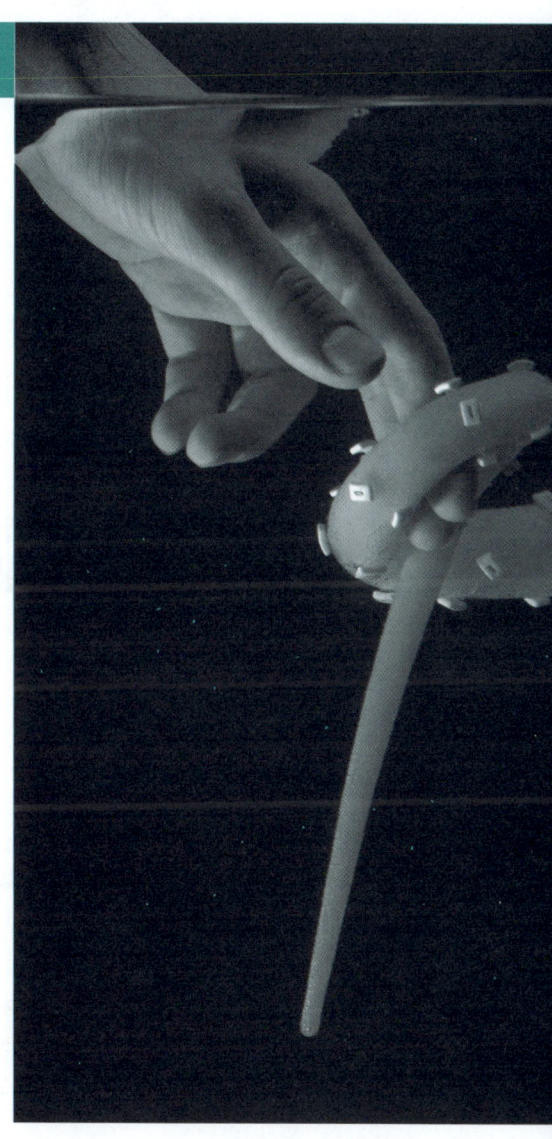

4 VOCABULARY: phrasal verbs

A Make phrasal verbs with the words from the box. Match them to the definitions.

| about | after | come | go | on | on | out | pick | point | rely | up |

1 to look for; chase: _____
2 to direct people's attention to something: _____
3 to learn: _____
4 to happen or occur: _____
5 to take place (leading to some result): _____
6 to have a dependence on: _____

B Complete the sentences using the phrasal verbs from Exercise A. Be sure to change the form where necessary.

1 One of the hopes for the next generation of Artificial Intelligence (AI) is that robots will _____ new skills by themselves, without being taught.
2 In his speech yesterday, the politician _____ that these technological advances would lead to more jobs, not fewer.
3 Technology is moving so fast. Who knows what will have _____ by the next century?
4 The robotics company _____ the most talented scientists, and that's why it was so successful.
5 I don't know what's _____ at that research institute, but I hear the strangest noises at night.
6 _____ too much _____ machines is risky. We shouldn't become too dependent.

5 GRAMMAR: future perfect progressive

A Put the words in the correct order to form sentences. Add commas if necessary.

1 we / been / for / 50 years / will / have / using / ~~2017~~ / ATM / ~~in~~ / machines
In 2017 _____.
2 been / ~~time~~ / I / teaching / ~~by~~ / I / will / for / retire / have / ~~the~~ / 20 years
By the time I _____.
3 when / for / ~~will~~ / leave / the / I / working / eight hours / have / I / office / been
I will _____.
4 ~~September~~ / house / have / ~~in~~ / 17 years / we / in / living / for / will / this / been
In September _____.

B Complete the sentences using the simple present or future perfect progressive form of the verb in parentheses.

1 By the end of next month, I _____ (study) robotics for a whole year.
2 By midnight, we _____ (play) this video game for seven hours.
3 When the bank _____ (replace) my lost ATM card, I _____ (wait) three weeks.
4 By the time the robot design _____ (come) out, he _____ (work) on it for a decade.
5 The factory _____ (use) those machines for just two years when the owner _____ (buy) the new ones.
6 By the end of this century, robots _____ (play) a part in our lives for years.

> **WATCH OUT!**
>
> (X) When I will have retired, I will have been working for 50 years.
>
> (✓) _____, I will have been working for 50 years.

6 WRITING: summarizing a text

A **Read the article and answer the question.**

According to the article, which of the following statements is false?

a) No robot has ever traveled further into the pyramid than the Djedi project robot.

b) The aim is to enter a room that has been unopened for thousands of years.

c) Robots have found the end of the Queen's tomb shaft twice before.

www.technewsdaily.com

HOME | CATEGORIES | LATEST | RECOMMENDED | MOST POPULAR   Search

ROBOT TO EXPOSE HIDDEN SECRETS OF THE PYRAMIDS

By Stuart Fox, TechNewsDaily Staff Writer   August 12 11:41 a.m. EST

Following in the footsteps of Howard Carter, a specialized robot has penetrated deeper into the Great Pyramid of Giza than ever before. The robot, part of an ongoing exploration called the Djedi Project, explored a shaft inaccessible to a previous robot, looking to unlock a room that has remained sealed for 4,500 years.

The robot explorer, built by researchers at Leeds University, England, in collaboration with French company Dassault Systèmes, and British robotics company Scoutek, incorporates a small fiber-optic camera for looking around corners, an ultrasonic probe for testing the quality of the rock, and a releasable mini-robot that can fit through spaces as small as 1.8 cm in diameter.

The robot traveled down a shaft located in the tomb of the Queen. This was the third time a robot has tried to find the end of the Queen's tomb shaft. The first expedition found that a giant stone door blocked the tunnel, and the second robot discovered another door behind that one. With its microbot and drill, the Leeds University researchers designed this new robot specifically to breach those obstacles.

The project is ongoing, but so far the robot has discovered small markings on the walls of the small passage leading to the Queen's chamber. It is thought these red marks could be examples of ancient graffiti by workers or hieroglyphs of religious importance. It is hoped these will provide some clues as to why the shafts were constructed in the first place.

RECOMMEND | SHARE | PRINT | SIGN UP FOR NEWSLETTER

B **Circle the following information in the article.**

- the title of the article
- the author's name
- the source of the article
- the date of the article

C **Decide if the following are main ideas (MI), relevant supporting information (RSI), or irrelevant information (II) for a summary. Write MI, RSI, or II after each sentence.**

1 This has been done before by Howard Carter. ___

2 This is the third attempt to reach the end of the Queen's tomb shaft. ___

3 The robot is especially designed to fit into very tight spaces. ___

4 Previous attempts found large doors blocking the way. ___

5 The robot has a fiber-optic camera, ultrasonic probe, and releasable mini-robot. ___

6 The robot will travel very deep in the Great Pyramid of Giza. ___

7 The robot was built in England. ___

8 The room at the end of the Queen's tomb has been closed for thousands of years. ___

9 The red marks might have religious importance, or could just be ancient graffiti. ___

10 The robot can fit through spaces as small as 1.8 cm in diameter. ___

11 Small red marks have been found on the walls of the shaft. ___

D **Write the main ideas and relevant supporting information in the correct order to create an outline for a summary of the article.**

skillsStudio

A You are going to listen to a podcast about robot technology in the future. Below is some of the vocabulary from the podcast. Match the words (1–8) to their definitions (a–h).

1	disarm	a)	person who is an expert in their field
2	downside	b)	cautious or not trusting
3	innovation	c)	disadvantage, or negative aspect
4	pulse	d)	new idea, method, or product
5	ridiculous	e)	crazy
6	specialist	f)	sign of a heartbeat, usually checked on the neck or wrists
7	surgery	g)	take a weapon away, or remove a weapon's threat
8	suspicious	h)	type of medical operation

B 🎧 11 Listen to the podcast. Check the topics that Dr. Julia Langham mentions.

Robots that check your health ☐   Robots that perform operations ☐
Robots that put out fires ☐   Robots that find bombs ☐
Robots that control household appliances ☐   Robots that educate people ☐
Robots that drive cars ☐   Robots that help fight crime ☐

C Listen again and choose the correct option to answer the questions.

1 Dr. Langham is a specialist in what area?
  a) automatics
  b) automobiles
  c) automation
  d) autographs

2 What is her current job primarily focused on?
  a) research
  b) robot design
  c) robot construction
  d) profit

3 How do robots help in the fight against crime, according to Dr. Langham?
  a) They disarm police.
  b) They locate criminals.
  c) They carry police equipment.
  d) They use force against the criminals.

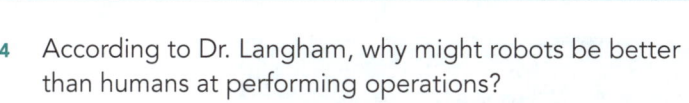

4   According to Dr. Langham, why might robots be better than humans at performing operations?
   a)   Human hands might move.
   b)   Robots can focus more on the job.
   c)   Patients prefer to be operated on by robots.
   d)   Doctors do not like invasive surgery.
5   What does Dr. Langham not say about robotic animals?
   a)   They can check that you are healthy.
   b)   They know if you've had an accident.
   c)   They understand how you're feeling.
   d)   They help with the housework.
6   Which of the following statements is false?
   a)   Dr. Langham thinks innovation may be limited in the next 10 years.
   b)   Dr. Langham thinks every innovation has possibilities.
   c)   Dr. Langham views technological advancement positively.
   d)   Dr. Langham thinks robots will be increasingly used in the military.

D   Listen again and complete the sentences from the podcast with the correct phrasal verb or future perfect verb.

1   … more and more police forces are starting to use robots to _____ their everyday crime fighting.
2   It is said that in 10 or 15 years, significant improvements _____ in the field of surgery using robots.
3   People sometimes _____ the ridiculous nature of certain innovations.
4   But these robots can actually _____ your moods and feelings.

E   Do you agree or disagree with the statement below? Provide context for your view, together with supporting reasons. Then look at counter-arguments and respond to them. Write 200–250 words.

"It is dangerous to rely too much on robots."

UNIT 7 THE CRITICAL CONSUMER

1 READING: understanding explanations and examples

A Read the article and check the best heading.

1. ☐ Knowing how food companies advertise their products
2. ☐ Learning the shopping habits of a supermarket customer
3. ☐ Understanding the tricks of the supermarket trade

HOME	ABOUT	TIPS	FORUM

¹ There's a reason your mother told you to make a grocery list and stick to it. Every part of the supermarket from parking lot to checkout counter is designed to make you spend more money and buy more food than you need. Customers may go to the store for milk and come away with a pint of ice cream (it was on sale), a fresh loaf of bread (it smelled so good), and a magazine (Jennifer is dating who?!). Altogether the supermarket is retail nirvana.

² **(1)** _____ flowers and fresh bread. Most supermarkets put these high profit departments near the front door, so you encounter them when your cart is empty and your spirits are high. Another reason to start with the floral display and baked goods is the smell. It activates your senses and makes you more likely to make unplanned purchases. **(2)** _____ it puts you in a good mood and makes you more willing to spend.

³ Supermarkets hide dairy products on the back wall and spread other essentials out around the store. **(3)** _____ you have to go through the whole store to get to them. And once customers start walking through the aisles, they are conditioned to walk up and down each one without deviating.

⁴ The items the store really wants you to buy are at eye level, **(4)** _____ where people are most likely to see them. In the cereal aisle, for instance, expensive brand name cereal is at eye level and favored items are placed at the end of aisles. Bulk cereal, however, is placed at the bottom and healthy cereal is at the top. And then there's kid's eye level. This is where you'll find sugary cereal and other items a kid will grab and beg his parents to buy.

⁵ Size and decoration also matter. In crowded stores, people spend less time shopping, **(5)** _____ they do less unplanned shopping, purchase fewer items, are less social and more nervous. Colors can also affect the way people shop. **(6)** _____ orange, which attracts people to a store and blue which encourages higher sales.

⁶ Hear that music? Studies have shown that people take their time and spend more money when hearing slow music, whereas loud music makes them move through the store quickly without affecting sales. And classical music, **(7)** _____ pieces by Mozart, leads people to buy more expensive products.

⁷ Of course, the most profitable area of the store is the checkout line. While standing in line, you will soon give in to temptation and buy something from the candy rack or the magazine you've been leafing through. And when it's time to present your Valued Shopper card, **(8)** _____ gives you the occasional deal and keeps you a regular customer for the store, the company gets to collect valuable shopping data about you.

From www.businessinsider.com

B Complete the article in Exercise A with the words and phrases from the box.

examples include   or   such as   take   the implication of this is that   what this means is   which   which means that

C Read the article in Exercise A again. Complete each statement with two words from the text.

1. When people are feeling positive, they tend to make a higher number of _____
2. To reach everyday items, it is necessary to walk through the _____
3. Important items are put on shelves which are at _____
4. In busy supermarkets, customers buy _____
5. A shopper card encourages you to be a _____

2 GRAMMAR: reduced adverb time clauses

A Match the rules (1–2) to the examples (a–b).

1   Delete the subject and verb *be*. _____
2   Delete the subject and change the verb to *-ing*. _____
a) People spend more money when they hear slow music.
    → People spend more money when hearing slow music.
b) While you are standing in line, you'll soon give in to temptation.
    → While standing in line, you'll soon give in to temptation.

B Read the forum page. Rewrite the underlined phrases (1–6) as reduced adverb time clauses.

| HOME | ABOUT | TIPS | **FORUM** | November 22, 5.04 |

MizT	I love shopping, but I worry about how much I spend. How can I make sure I don't buy much **(1)** <u>when I'm shopping</u>?
BigTeen	**(2)** <u>Before you go</u> to the supermarket, write a list of everything you need. **(3)** <u>When you walk</u> around the supermarket, make sure you buy only the things on the list. You'll see a huge drop in your food bill, promise!
Over8Ted	**(4)** <u>Before you buy</u> food, why don't you compare prices online? **(5)** <u>After you see</u> which one has the best offers, you'll know where to go.
Lily12	Don't be fooled by the tricks supermarkets use **(6)** <u>while you are shopping</u>. Offers usually don't save you money at all.

1 _____   3 _____   5 _____
2 _____   4 _____   6 _____

WATCH OUT!

✗ While paying at the checkout, a store assistant finished packing my bags.

✓ While _____ paying at the checkout, a store assistant finished packing my bags.

3 VOCABULARY: adjectives ending in *–able/–ible*

A 🎧 12 Listen to eight definitions. Number the words to match them to their definitions.

a) ☐ accountable   d) ☐ disposable   g) ☐ recyclable
b) ☐ affordable   e) ☐ edible   h) ☐ returnable
c) ☐ biodegradable   f) ☐ perishable

B Complete the text with the words from Exercise A.

THE ECO ♻ WARRIOR

How could our local supermarkets be more **(1)** _____ for their impact on the environment? Well, they could reduce the number of special offers of **(2)** _____ goods which simply increase waste, as such goods are **(3)** _____, and shoppers often find they cannot eat them before their use-by date. They could also make eco-friendly products more **(4)** _____ so more customers would buy them. Offering paper bags at the checkout is preferable to plastic ones which are not **(5)** _____ and can therefore take up to twenty years to break down. However, supermarkets could also encourage manufacturers to use more **(6)** _____ packaging and less **(7)** _____ packaging that is simply thrown away after it is opened. They could also highlight to customers which bottles are **(8)** _____ for recycling, so customers can make the best environmental choice.

4 GRAMMAR: reduced adverb cause-effect clauses

A Complete the sentences with *being*, *having*, or *wanting*.

1 _____ to shop more ethically, she stopped going to supermarkets.

2 Not _____ tried the food, I couldn't comment on the restaurant.

3 _____ biodegradable, these diapers are environmentally friendly.

B Choose the correct option to complete the sentences.

1 *Having had moved house* / *Having moved house* before, I knew what to expect.

2 *Being returnable* / *Because being returnable*, glass bottles are a better option than plastic.

3 *Not understanding* / *Not having understanding* that fruit is biodegradable, people throw it in the trash.

4 *Stores are* / *Stores, being* more environmentally aware, are selling fewer disposable items.

5 *Because knowing* / *Knowing* we would be accountable for our actions, we didn't break the rules.

6 *Not wanted* / *Not wanting* to spend a lot of money, we furnished our home with second-hand furniture.

> ### WATCH OUT!
> ✗ Wanting not to spend too much money, I bought the cheaper T-shirt.
>
> ✓ _____ to spend too much money, I bought the cheaper T-shirt.

C Complete the article with the correct form of the words from the box.

be	do	earn	know	learn	own

MOVING HOME | BUYING YOUR FIRST HOME | RENTING YOUR FIRST HOME

Renting my first apartment could have been really costly. **(1)** _____ no furniture at all, my first thought was to rent a furnished place. However, **(2)** _____ how much more expensive that can be, a friend suggested I rent an unfurnished apartment and furnish it with old, pre-loved furniture being given away locally for free. After a few weeks, **(3)** _____ some research, I realized he was right. So, I went for an unfurnished apartment in a nice part of the city. Not **(4)** _____ a lot of money, I had to swap my skills for the skills of some of my friends to get it looking right. For example, I asked a friend to turn some old material into curtains, not **(5)** _____ able to sew at all myself, in exchange for guitar lessons. And **(6)** _____ how to cook a pretty mean steak, I asked a friend with a van to pick up the furniture in exchange for a three-course meal. In the end, I had a great apartment that looked fantastic, and yet, cost me next to nothing.

5 COMMUNICATION STRATEGY: modifying a statement

A Match the two parts to make phrases to modify statements.

1 But then   a) actually,

2 That   b) said that,

3 Although   c) about it,

4 On second   d) said,

5 Having   e) again,

6 Having thought   f) thought

B  **13 Listen to Mira and Sam. Decide if each statement is T (true) or F (false).**

1 Mira is a shopaholic who is in debt.   T / F
2 Mira doesn't get any joy from shopping.   T / F
3 Mira's never been shopping without buying something.   T / F
4 Sam ends up suggesting she try to limit what she spends. T / F

C Listen again. Complete the sentences with the phrases from Exercise A.

1 Well, I'm not broke. _____, if I don't do something, I may be soon.
2 _____, I did realize it, but I didn't want to accept it.
3 Of course, _____, I don't feel so good when I see my credit card statement.
4 _____, I haven't tried that, so I can't say for sure.
5 You know, _____, I don't see the point.
6 _____ how about trying to stick to an affordable budget first?

6 VOCABULARY: money and finances

A Put the letters in parentheses in the correct order to complete the phrases.

1 to _____ on expenses (*tcu wodn*)
2 to buy something on _____ (*tidcer*)
3 to be _____ (*kebor*)
4 to _____ to a plan (*kicst*)
5 to _____ your money (*trschet*)
6 to be able to _____ something (*ofradf*)
7 to buy something _____ (*no esla*)
8 to stick to a _____ (*gtdueb*)

B Complete the blog with words and phrases from Exercise A.

BLOGtime

FEATURES **BLOG** JOIN LOGIN

Posted by BenW on January 16

Ben Webb Feels Consumer Gloom

Do you usually make sure you can **(1)** _____ something before buying it? Very wise. I don't, which is why I'm always **(2)** _____. While walking down the street, I check out store windows for anything on **(3)** _____, ready to swoop in and buy it on **(4)** _____. This is in stark contrast to a guy I met this week who's living an anti-consumer lifestyle. He grows his own vegetables, makes his own jam, swaps these for meat from a local farmer, gets any household items and furniture for free from people online, and uses solar power to heat his home. This is the perfect way to **(5)** _____ your money or, better yet, not spend any. Living his life in this way, there's no need for him to **(6)** _____ on expenses because he doesn't really have any! But I don't know. Although I find it tough to try to stick to a **(7)** _____ of $20 a day, I don't think I'm ready to go as far as growing my own food yet.

COMMENT REBLOG FAVORITE EMAIL RECOMMEND PRINT

skillsStudio

A Read the blog entry on page 45. Check the correct description.

1 ☐ The text argues in favor of conscious consumerism.
2 ☐ The text argues against conscious consumerism.
3 ☐ The text presents a neutral account of conscious consumerism.

B Complete the summary with one, two, or three words from the blog entry.

Before the writer started her blog, she bought anything she wanted, with little (1) _____ for social, personal, or environmental issues. She paid little attention to the quantity of items she bought, (2) _____ other things such as the ingredients or packaging. However, through education her purchasing habits changed. Since then she has (3) _____ fair trade, organic, and safe products and built an online shop selling such products.

At first, the writer had (4) _____ for products which didn't reach the standards she'd set herself, but living her life this way needed a lot of (5) _____. She also realized some of her actions weren't (6) _____, such as not letting her little sister buy bottled water when thirsty. So now, she occasionally buys some products which aren't fair trade, organic, or environmentally safe because without them she'd find it difficult to live her life in a (7) _____ manner. She believes the key things are that we make (8) _____ decisions, know what effect these decisions have, (9) _____ so that other people are educated and attempt to change (10) _____.

C Read the blog entry in Exercise A again. Decide if each statement is T (true), F (false), or NM (not mentioned).

1 Before her blog, the writer thought carefully if she wanted a product before buying it.   T / F / NM
2 The writer began to read up on products before buying them.   T / F / NM
3 On the writer's website, you can exchange unwanted products.   T / F / NM
4 The writer only bought clothes made by workers who worked in good conditions.   T / F / NM
5 The writer's strict standards led to logical thought that was good for everyone.   T / F / NM
6 The writer jokes that her decisions have resulted in a family member needing professional help.   T / F / NM
7 The writer uses only hygiene products without chemicals.   T / F / NM
8 The writer tries to educate people she knows to buy less damaging personal products.   T / F / NM
9 The writer believes she should always follow a conscious consumerist lifestyle or not bother at all.   T / F / NM
10 The writer says we should show admiration for organizations that help us be conscious consumers.   T / F / NM

D You're studying at an international college. You have received the following email from the principal, Mr. Jones. Write a proposal using your notes on the email to help you. Write between 220 and 260 words.

> **From:** principal@internationalcoll.com   **Date:** May 17
> **Subject:** Becoming a more conscious consumer
>
> We're looking at making the college a more conscious consumer and would love you to write a proposal, giving us suggestions on how we can do this. Perhaps you could think about our classrooms, library, store, and cafeteria.
>
> Use recycled paper.   More recycling bins.   Sell fair trade goods.   Change to organic food.

By now, from my blog, you probably know that I was not always a conscious consumer. To be precise, in the days before this blog, I was quite an unconscious consumer. I used to shop for anything, anytime, with little to no regard for the environmental, personal health, or social impact of my purchases. I didn't think about how much I was buying, let alone what the product was made of, how its ingredients might affect me or my surroundings, how it was packaged, and whether or not I really needed the product. It may be hard to believe, but this environmental supporter was at one time a greedy consumer.

After quite a lot of soul searching and, of course, a ton of awareness and education, I changed my wasteful ways and started buying less, researching the environmental and personal impact of my potential purchases, and understanding the social conditions of the workers who make the products I buy. I have spoken up for fair trade clothing, jewelry and food, safe cosmetics, organic clothing and food, non-toxic cleaning products and housewares extensively. While building my online shop, I have selected all these types of products, along with those made of recycled materials—old, unwanted items which have been upcycled into new, beautiful and useful goods—and products that are made with environmental, socially responsible, and health conscious practices in mind.

For a while after my "conversion," I had zero tolerance for anything that did not meet my new standards. (What can I say? I'm a very passionate person!) I would laugh disrespectfully at anyone who bought bottled water. I stopped buying anything I didn't truly need, bought only organic produce and meats, and used personal care products made with only the most natural and toxin-free ingredients. I even made sure that my clothing was not made in sweatshops in developing countries or put together by the hand of a child.

Unfortunately, living this way is not very convenient and requires a lot of sacrifice. At times I became so obsessed with doing the 'right thing', that I was no longer thinking clearly and I let it negatively affect others and not just myself. For example, if I was out with my little sister and we forgot to bring water (in a reusable bottle of course), and my sister was thirsty, I refused to let her buy bottled water even if we couldn't find a water fountain or tap water nearby. My poor baby sister had to go without drinking. What?? That's not rational. Our planet's plastic trash problem is not going to be affected one way or another by my occasional purchase of water in a plastic bottle that can later be recycled (but my sister will probably be in therapy for a long time). So I started to relax my rules a little bit.

For example, I haven't found a natural deodorant that I feel is strong enough for me. So rather than smell like a gym locker all day and lose friends, I use an antiperspirant product that may be causing harm to my body and sending toxins into the water supply. (Feel free to send me suggestions for a strong natural deodorant that works really well!)

I don't say anything to my friends when I stay with them for the weekend and they supply me with shampoo and conditioner that contain some harmful chemicals. I realize that our friendship is important and a few days of using that stuff is not going to kill me. Besides, it's my fault for forgetting to take my own.

When I see that adorable sweater in the boutique window that fits perfectly and looks good with jeans, I may buy it even if it is not made of organic cotton or does not carry the fair trade label. Also, I still use disposable tissues as I find hankies quite disgusting. You get the point.

If I didn't allow myself these transgressions, I might find it hard to continue with my more conscious lifestyle, give it up altogether, and (hopefully not!) go back to my wasteful ways from before this blog. What's important is that we make well-informed decisions and understand the impact of our purchases on our health, the environment, and social justice. We should try hard to do the best we can. We should spread the word, get involved, and try to change regulation and policy. And, of course, celebrate all the great companies that make it easier rather than harder for us to make better choices.

Adapted from www.ecoplum.com

UNIT 8 ARTISTIC LICENSE

1 LISTENING: inferring factual information

Henri Matisse

Georges Braque

A))) **14** Listen to a tour guide showing tourists around an art museum. Match each artist (1–6) to the style associated with him (a–f).

1	Henri Matisse	a)	Abstract Expressionism
2	Edvard Munch	b)	Fauvism
3	Georges Braque	c)	Pop Art
4	Marcel Duchamp	d)	Dadaism
5	Mark Rothko	e)	Cubism
6	Andy Warhol	f)	Expressionism

B Listen again and choose the correct option to complete the sentences.

1 Louis Vauxcelles found the Fauvist paintings *fresh and exciting* / *too simple*.
2 The Expressionist artists *tried* / *didn't try* to accurately paint what they saw in front of them.
3 Dadaist artists were *in favor of* / *against* traditional art.
4 As Abstract Expressionism emerged, *Paris* / *New York* was a dangerous place.
5 The guide *thinks* / *doesn't think* Rothko's art is abstract.
6 Pop Art was very *similar to* / *different from* Abstract Expressionism.

2 VOCABULARY: describing art

A Choose the correct word to complete the sentences below.

1 Magritte was a leading light in the Surrealist *school* / *symbol* of painting.
2 Although Henri Rousseau's style was regarded as *in proportion* / *unconventional* during his lifetime, it was later very influential.
3 The Dadaists were *illustrative* / *controversial*, provoking strong opinions both in favor of and against them.
4 The *concept* / *illustration* of Expressionist art was to display the artists' feelings and emotions.
5 Abstract Expressionists' art *represents* / *schools* their emotions. You can almost feel the passion on the canvas.
6 The Dadaist movement became a *symbol* / *proportion* of anti-establishment sentiment.
7 The artist emphasizes the main subject matter beautifully. Can you see how it is not *in proportion* / *symbolic* to the rest of the painting?
8 The Pop Artists are a good *controversy* / *illustration* of how art and popular culture could be combined.

B Complete the TV guide with the correct form of words from Exercise A.

TV TONIGHT

Tonight's show on Pablo Picasso is quite enlightening. He is shown to be a somewhat (1) _____ figure, drawing great praise from some and strong criticism from others—one renowned journalist described him as just "a big show-off." But, love him or hate him, you cannot deny his influence. As well as co-founding the Cubist (2) _____ of art, he had connections with most of the other artistic styles of the 20th Century. In some ways he was (3) _____. For example, his 1907 work *Les Demoiselles d'Avignon* broke tradition by not having a three-dimensional perspective and not being in perfect (4) _____. But despite the eccentric (5) _____ of some of his work, he was in other ways quite the opposite: conformist—some would even say predictable. I did also learn something about his most famous mural, *Guernica*, with its blending of modern and traditional images—a perfect (6) _____ of how art can become an anti-war (7) _____. I didn't know, for example, that the light bulb (*bombilla* in Spanish) was intended to (8) _____ a bomb (*bomba*). Even though there seems to be a trend these days toward revealing the darker side of the man, this show is still worth watching.

3 GRAMMAR: inverted conditionals

A Put the words in the correct order to form sentences.

1 not sold / had he / have given up / he might / his first painting, / .

_____

2 he would / the artist / lived longer, / had / many more masterpieces / have produced / .

_____

3 this art course, / be sure / should / every class / you take / to attend / .

_____

4 you want to be / be prepared / for little financial gain / to work hard / should / an artist, / .

_____

5 gone to Paris, / have met / had Van Gogh not / he wouldn't / the artist Gauguin / .

_____

6 we would have gone / had we known / to see the exhibition / how talented he was, / sooner / .

_____

B There is one mistake in each sentence. Rewrite the sentences correctly.

1 Had the concept have been clearer, more people might have appreciated the work.

_____
_____

2 Should you decided to display this controversial work, you will likely get many complaints.

_____

3 Hadn't the artist included such strong symbols in his paintings, the impact would have been reduced.

_____

4 Should you tried a more conventional approach, perhaps the establishment would have been more welcoming of your work.

_____

5 Should the images are out of proportion, you might have to start again.

_____

> ## WATCH OUT!
>
> ✗ Hadn't she become a lawyer, she would have been an artist.
>
> ✓ _____ become a lawyer, she would have been an artist.

4 VOCABULARY: negative prefixes un-, non-, mis-, im-, in-

A Complete the sentences using the correct prefixes.

1 This is a rather _____ traditional style of painting, but it appeals to many artists—both beginner and experienced.

2 Should you be _____ able to take the test on that day, contact me and we'll schedule another time.

3 Many people found his opinions controversial, but I think he was just _____ understood

4 Had he been _____ willing to help, the project would never have even gotten started.

5 It's _____ comprehensible to me that anyone would pay such a large sum of money just for a painting.

6 I find his work both _____ original and uninspiring.

7 It's almost _____ visible to the naked eye, but with a magnifying glass you can clearly see the artist's initials at the bottom.

8 The huge marble statue is incredibly heavy. I think it's _____ movable unless you use some machinery to help you.

B Complete the article using the correct adjectives.

GANG WARFARE

There's always one school of artists who are **(1)** *unable / incomprehensible* or **(2)** *unwilling / mismatched* to accept another school. Take the Stuckists, a group of figurative artists who have chosen to reject conceptual art, labeling it as **(3)** *invisible / uninteresting* and too **(4)** *immovable / incomprehensible*. And with over 200 groups in nearly 50 countries, it's **(5)** *impossible / non-standard* to ignore the Stuckists. Conceptual artists have tried, as have Surrealists, who have denounced them as childish. "It's incredible to think that some people don't like us. We're just **(6)** *unloving / misunderstood*," said a Stuckist spokesperson, who looked anything but surprised. Or upset for that matter.

THE STUCKISTS
www.stuckism.com
THE
TURNER
PRIZE
IS
DEAD

5 GRAMMAR: adjective phrase + indirect question

WATCH OUT!

(✗) It's difficult to know will people like her work.

(✓) It's difficult to know _____ _____ like her work.

A Rewrite the direct questions as indirect questions, using the prompts and the words in parentheses.

1 Where did this trend start?
It's _____. *(difficult/know)*

2 How did he achieve such an intricate effect?
It's _____. *(not easy/tell)*

3 Who did you think would see this graffiti?
It's _____. *(important/you/explain)*

B Rewrite the following as direct questions.

1 It would be good to find out where I can see interesting exhibitions this weekend.

2 It would be interesting to know whether the sculpture took a long time to complete.

3 It's difficult for me to understand why so many people like this sort of art.

4 It's impossible to tell who sculpted this.

5 It's hard for me to give an opinion about how much this painting would have cost 20 years ago.

6 WRITING: a review

A Number the paragraphs of the review in the correct order (1–4).

a) ____ Although the material appears removed from its natural context, and some is not very smart, this is an outstanding exhibition, and I would have no hesitation in recommending it to all.

b) ____ However, there are many things I really liked about it. First, the venue is an excellent choice. Choosing a warehouse with huge brick walls is unconventional, but ideal for a graffiti artist. I also liked the symbolism in his work. He has a live elephant painted in the colors of his themed living room, which represents important issues in the world, such as poverty. Finally, I loved his recurring motif of rats, which represent for him the triumph of the downtrodden people.

c) ____ Barely Legal is the first large scale U.S. exhibition of British street artist Banksy's work. It is taking place at the Downtown L.A. Warehouse from Friday, September 15.

d) ____ There are some aspects of the exhibition I found a little disappointing. First, the context of street art is the street. Although it would be hard to display all of his pieces outside, it would have been nice for some of the work to be set on the street. Second, his material is in the most part anarchic, ironic, and amusing, but I found some of it childish, with some images clearly designed just to shock.

B Put the introduction and main body of a concert review in the correct order.

a) ☐ What's more, if I pay that much money, I expect to be entertained for at least a couple of hours. However, the band played for only 50 minutes. That was a real disappointment.

b) ☐ Also, some bands only play their new songs— which can be disappointing—but I'm happy to say that the Hi-Fi Kings played all of their classics.

c) ☐ There were certainly some positives to take away from the experience. Firstly, the sound engineers had done an amazing job of setting up the stage, with the result that these clearly talented musicians sounded amazing.

d) ☐ However, there were also a couple of serious negatives. For example, the cost of the tickets was shocking. I remember when you could see your favorite bands for less than 20 bucks, but a ticket for this concert was $150—and the seat wasn't even in a good spot.

e) ☐ On Saturday September 24, I was able to view their concert along with 30,000 fans at the Hollywood Bowl.

f) ☐ The Hi-Fi Kings are currently in the middle of their nationwide tour.

C Look at the two conclusions below. Choose the one that is more suitable for the review.

a) I like this band, and they played a concert on September 24 in Hollywood. I thought the tickets were expensive, and I wish they had played longer. However, there was a really good sound, and they played lots of my favorite songs. It was fun dancing to their music.

b) All in all, I thought the concert was a let down. Although I enjoyed listening to some good songs, and the sound quality was good, I thought the cost of the tickets was far too much. Also, if I'm spending that amount of money, I expect them to play for much longer. It wasn't terrible, but I still wouldn't recommend others to see this band.

skillsStudio

A Match the words (1–8) to their definitions (a–h).

1. a person receiving treatment
2. not using words or speech
3. facts or information to prove that something is true
4. a form of treatment for someone with mental health issues or emotional problems
5. relating to or affecting the mind
6. being skilled at something
7. having no value or purpose
8. deep and clinical unhappiness

a) depression
b) evidence
c) patient
d) pointless
e) proficient
f) psychological
g) therapy
h) non-verbal

B 🎧 **15** Which of the following do you think best describes art therapy? Listen to a lecture and Q&A session about art therapy, and check your answer.

a) treatment that cures severe diseases through learning about art
b) treatment where patients express and explore themselves through creating art
c) treatment where patients feel better by looking at famous works of art

C Listen again and choose the correct option, a, b, c, or d.

1. For approximately how long has art therapy been a true profession?
   a) thousands of years
   b) hundreds of years
   c) a hundred years
   d) 60 or 70 years
2. In his introduction, what does Dr. Bergmann not say art therapy can help patients achieve?
   a) awareness of their character
   b) awareness of their actions
   c) awareness of their artistic ability
   d) awareness of their problems
3. According to Dr. Bergmann, what is an additional proven effect of art therapy?
   a) It dismisses patients' suffering.
   b) It can reduce tiredness among cancer patients.
   c) It can raise depression among cancer patients.
   d) It can help cure cancer.
4. What does Dr. Bergmann say about the cost of art therapy?
   a) No health authorities cover the expense.
   b) No insurance providers cover the expense.
   c) It's more expensive than other forms of therapy.
   d) Different therapists charge different amounts.

5   What can you infer from Dr. Bergmann's reaction to the
    third speaker's question?
    a)   He doesn't think she understands this subject very well.
    b)   He thinks she asked an excellent question.
    c)   He has never heard this question before.
    d)   Most people understand art therapy very well.

6   What can you infer from Dr. Bergmann's answer to the fourth speaker's question?
    a)   Art therapy works for everybody.
    b)   Don't go to art therapy if you don't believe in it.
    c)   Art therapy is often a waste of time.
    d)   You need to be severely troubled to benefit from art therapy.

D   Listen again and complete the notes from the lecture.

Art Therapy – Dr. Bergmann Lecture
May 28

Art Therapy Overview

started to become a true profession from mid-(1) _____ Century
people can share deep, possibly hidden (2) _____
profound (3) _____ between patient and art therapist
patient can understand their personality, (4) _____, and issues

Art Therapy and Cancer

evidence that therapy helps cancer sufferers: can help with (5) _____
lower levels of (6) _____
assist in dealing with pain
improve overall quality of (7) _____

Cost

probably pay on an (8) _____ basis
can seem quite expensive
large commitment of time and (9) _____

For everybody?

struggle to get benefit if you are resistant
to art therapy e.g. don't believe in its
(10) _____

But...

many people develop a deep, understanding
(11) _____ with their therapist

**E   Read the statement. Do you agree or disagree? Use specific reasons
and examples to support your answer. Write 260–300 words.**

"Art therapy should be available, free of charge, to anybody who wants it."

UNIT 9 JUST PLAYING?

1 READING: understanding intent

A Read the texts (1–4) and match them to the writer's intent (a–e).
One option is not needed.

a) ☐ persuade   **b)** ☐ entertain   **c)** ☐ criticize   **d)** ☐ inform   **e)** ☐ compare

---

1

Monday, January 24   *5 Comments*

KIDS SAY SUCH FUNNY THINGS!
—————————————————————— *posted by Modern Mom*

So, four-year-old Brandon and I were sitting playing a game of Snap yesterday afternoon. As my regular readers know, he's not a good loser, so I was kind of letting him win—anything for an easy life! At the end, he turned around to me, patted me on the arm, and said, "Don't be sad, Mommy. It's not your fault you're not very good. Just remember, 'Practice makes perfect.'" I nearly died laughing!

2

Kidsplay

Home   About   Ideas   Forum

It seems that children all around the world enjoy a game of tag, but not all the games are exactly the same. When American children play, one child chases the other children until they catch one and trade places. However, in Saudi Arabia, all but one child—the hunter—hides and that child has to find the hiding places of the others before they catch them. This is similar to the German game, except there only one child hides and everyone else is the catcher. When a catcher finds the child hiding, they too have to hide in the same place. The last catcher to find the hiding place is the loser.

---

3 Sunday, March 4

THE SPORT

Baseball star Daniel Murphy has received criticism for missing a game in order to be at his wife's side as she gave birth. Radio hosts Mike Francesca and Boomer Esiason expressed dismay that Murphy took all three days of his paternity leave, missing two games instead of just one, and said they believed it was his obligation to play due to the salary he receives. Murphy defended himself by saying he felt it was right to be with his wife and child after the birth.

---

4 ## GAMES blog

HOME   FEATURES   NEWS   FORUM   REVIEWS

Strike while the iron's hot

Video games fans will finally get their hands on a copy of real-time strategy game *Iron Strategum* tomorrow. They'll discover a clever, unique game that offers a sensible balance between accessibility and depth of play. Graphically, the game never fails to impress with its ability to zoom in to appreciate finer detail, and the needless resource gathering associated with this type of game has been abandoned. With a thriving multi-player online community, its longevity is ensured, so this is clearly a good investment for all you serious gamers out there.

B Read each text in Exercise A again. Match each text (1–4) with the writer's intent.

a) the writer gives a balanced account of the facts ___

b) the writer gives a recommendation ___

c) the writer gives examples to highlight similarities/differences ___

d) the writer uses humor ___

2 VOCABULARY: childhood development

Complete the article with the words from the box.

emerge   engaging in   imitate   literacy   numeracy   open-ended   outcome   outlet

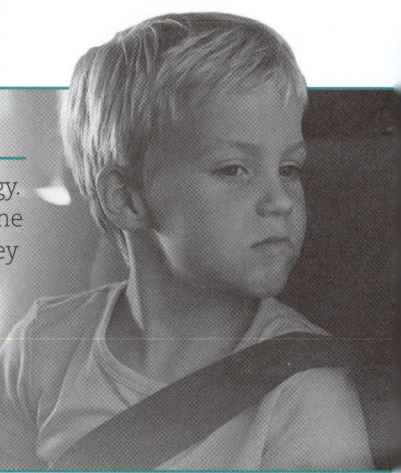

Are we there yet?

When driving with kids, it is often hard to find a good **(1)** _____ for their energy. Kids will **(2)** _____ you, so if you start shouting, so will they. **(3)** _____ the simplest of games can keep them happy. For older kids, the State Game (in which they try to find license plates on passing cars and as many as possible from their chosen U.S. state) helps to improve their **(4)** _____ , while the License Plate Numbers Game (they add up all the numbers on a license plate) does the same for their **(5)** _____ . Since these games are **(6)** _____ , the kids will keep playing until they've had enough without the need for a clear **(7)** _____ or an overall winner to **(8)** _____ .

3 GRAMMAR: the subjunctive

A Complete the sentences with the correct positive or negative form of the verb.

allow   have   keep   lose   protect   recommend   spend   stay

1 Experts say it's important that a child _____ inside all day.
2 They recommend that everyone _____ at least 30 minutes' of fresh air a day.
3 It's essential that a child _____ too much time in front of the TV.
4 Parents should insist that their child's school _____ children outside at recess.
5 It's recommended that a child _____ touch with nature.
6 Experts suggest that a parent _____ their child too much and let them take some risks.
7 Doctors ask that a child _____ fit through outside play.
8 We _____ that parents keep a child inside all winter as kids should play out every day.

WATCH OUT!

✗ She insisted that he stops playing football in the office.

✓ She insisted that he _____ playing football in the office.

B Complete the advertisement with the correct form of the phrases from the box. Three phrases are not needed.

a child not learn   a child take risks   children not grow up   don't propose
have   insist   not bring   your child develop   your child visit

It's important that **(1)** _____ without an understanding of the natural world, and our forest school makes that possible. Built on the edge of the Ashley forest, we offer the chance to learn, explore, and create. Experts recommend that **(2)** _____ while growing up and the forest allows them the chance to do just that, but in a safe environment. We **(3)** _____ that all our children spend all day outside of course, but a large portion of our time is spent in the forest working on a variety of projects. We recommend that **(4)** _____ us for a day* to learn more about the incredible work that we do. Call now to book a place!
*NB We ask that children **(5)** _____ toys with them but **(6)** _____ warm clothes with them instead.

4 VOCABULARY: making and responding to invitations

A Put the words in the correct order to make phrases.

1 like / would / try / to / you / out / it / ? _____
2 it / you / are / for / up / ? _____
3 love / yes, / to / I'd /. _____
4 can't / sorry, / it / do / . _____
5 I / a / check / take / can / rain / ? _____
6 go / to / want / ? _____

B Write the correct number of each phrase from Exercise A to complete the conversation.

Jalil: Hey, Daisy. A few people from our class are thinking of hanging out at the lake this afternoon. **(a)** _____?

Daisy: **(b)** _____. I have to pick my sister up from the station. She's visiting for a few days.

Jalil: No problem. Oh, there's a new club opening downtown on Saturday. **(c)** _____?

Daisy: I would, but my sister's kind of shy, so I don't think it'd be her scene. **(d)** _____?

Jalil: Sure. Hey, do you like rock music?

Daisy: Yeah, I love it.

Jalil: There's a Thrillers concert here next month, and I've got two extra tickets. **(e)** _____?

Daisy: I certainly am! **(f)** _____! I'll ask Tom if he wants to go! Oh, thanks, Jalil. You're the best!

Jalil: What …? Oh, sure.

5 COMMUNICATION STRATEGY: making and responding to invitations

A 》》16 Listen to three conversations. Check whether the invitation is accepted or declined in each conversation.

1 ☐ accepted   ☐ declined
2 ☐ accepted   ☐ declined
3 ☐ accepted   ☐ declined

B Look at the phrases in Section 4, Exercise A. Listen again and write the numbers of the phrases used in each conversation.

Conversation 1: _____   Conversation 2: _____   Conversation 3: _____

6 GRAMMAR: alternatives to the subjunctive

A Match the two parts to make complete sentences.

1 Some doctors insist …
2 For example, they suggest …
3 People enjoy different activities, so they say it's good …
4 To keep our mind and body healthy, they recommend …
5 They ask us …
6 We all lose brain cells when we get older, so they propose …

a) learning a foreign language to help increase brain power.
b) starting to exercise our brains in our 20s or 30s, to minimize the effect of aging.
c) to reduce the stress in our lives.
d) their patients learn how to train their brains better.
e) to try different techniques to improve our memories.
f) doing regular exercise.

B Choose the correct option to complete the sentences.

1 It is important *exercise / to exercise* our brains regularly.
2 Some companies suggest *playing / to play* brain training games.
3 Brain training games demand that you *concentrate / concentrating* hard.
4 It is best for you *doing / to do* challenging tasks that you can finally achieve.
5 Some people have suggested *doing / to do* brain training games to increase your intelligence.
6 They insist that you *play / playing* them every day.

C Complete the article with the correct form of the verb in parentheses. Choose the infinitive, *to* + infinitive or gerund.

WATCH OUT!

✗ I recommend him to play this game.

✓ I recommend that he _____ this game.

✓ I recommend _____ this game.

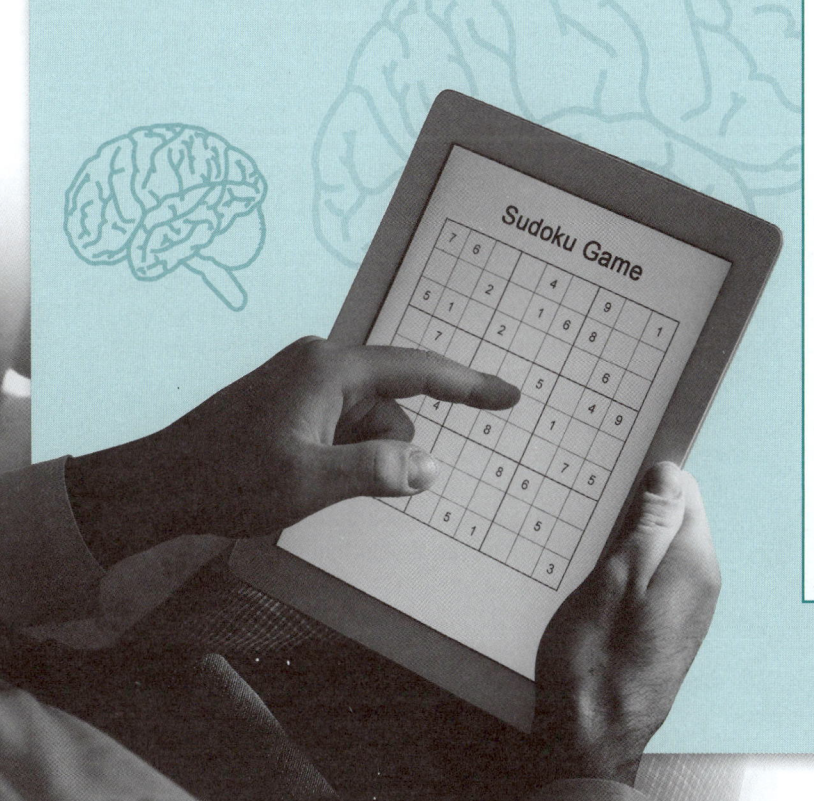

A recent study on the effectiveness of brain-training games saw neuroscientist Dr. Adrian Owen divide over 11,000 18–60 year-olds into three groups. He asked group 1 **(1)** _____ (*complete*) a simple fact-finding task. He asked that group 2 **(2)** _____ (*do*) more difficult reasoning and problem-solving tests. He requested that group 3 **(3)** _____ (*work*) on specific brain-training games which required **(4)** _____ (*process*) information more carefully than Groups 1 or 2.

Prior to the experiment, one or two experts had insisted that everyone **(5)** _____ (*play*) brain-training games to increase their brain function. However, the results showed that by repeating the same tasks several times, Groups 1 and 2 had improved in those tasks, but there was no sign of improvement in brain function. Surprisingly, exactly the same applied to Group 3, leading the researchers to conclude that brain-training games don't work. Dr. Owen proposes **(6)** _____ (*do*) more tests like this in future to check claims such as those made about brain-training games.

Information source: www.nature.com

skillsStudio

A Read the article and answer the question.

What is the writer's intention: to entertain, inform, or persuade? _____

THE IMPORTANCE OF
PLAY
FOR ADULTS

Our society tends to dismiss play for adults. Play is **(a)** <u>perceived as unproductive</u>, not worth worrying about or even as **(b)** <u>a guilty pleasure</u>. The notion is that once we reach adulthood, it's time to get serious, and between personal and professional responsibilities, there's no time to play. "The only kind [of play] we honor is competitive play," according to Bowen F. White, a medical doctor and author of *Why Normal Isn't Healthy*. But play is just as essential for adults as it is for kids. Play brings joy. And it's vital for problem solving, creativity, and relationships.

1 _____

Brown has spent decades studying the power of play in everyone from prisoners to business people to artists and Nobel Prize winners. He's reviewed over 6,000 "play histories," or case studies, that explore the role of play in each person's childhood and adulthood.

2 _____

Play can even **(c)** <u>facilitate deep connections</u> between strangers and **(d)** <u>cultivate healing</u>. In addition to being a doctor and speaker, Dr. White is a clown. Over two decades ago, White began working with **(e)** <u>legendary physician</u> and clown, Patch Adams, who was the focus of a 1998 film of the same name.

3 _____

He's clowned on the streets of Moscow. And even though he doesn't speak Russian, that didn't stop him from playing with people in Red Square. Within 45 minutes, he was juggling and joking with a crowd of 30.

4 _____

As White said, play can lead us to these sacred spaces and **(f)** <u>touch people</u> in powerful ways. Of course we don't need to play every second of the day to enjoy play's benefits. In his book, Brown calls play **(g)** <u>a catalyst for positivity.</u> A little bit of play, he writes, can go a long way toward **(h)** <u>boosting our productivity</u> and happiness. So how can you add play into your life? Here are a few tips from the experts.

5 _____

You could try thinking back to your past. In his book, Brown includes instructions to help readers reconnect with play. He suggests readers mine their past for play memories. What did you do as a child that excited you? Did you engage in those activities alone or with others? Or both? How can you recreate that today?

6 _____

And of course, playing with kids helps us experience the magic of play **(i)** <u>through their perspective</u>. White and Brown both talked about playing around with their grandkids. So, any time you think play is a waste, remember that it offers some **(j)** <u>serious benefits</u> for both you and others. As Brown says in his book, "Play is the purest expression of love."

From http://psychcentral.com

B Read the article again. Match the underlined expressions (a–j) to their meanings (1–10).

1   Affect people's emotions: _____
2   Understood to not achieve any benefits: _____
3   Something that creates a good feeling: _____
4   From someone else's viewpoint: _____
5   Increasing the amount of benefits achieved: _____
6   Develop the process of getting healthy again: _____
7   Important advantages: _____
8   Make stronger relationships possible: _____
9   Something that makes you happy but you feel ashamed about it: _____
10 Famous doctor: _____

**C Six paragraphs have been taken out of the article in Exercise A.
Choose one (A–G) to fit each gap in the article. One paragraph is not needed.**

> **A** Well, a first step is to change how you think about play. Remember that play is important for all aspects of our lives, including creativity and relationships. Give yourself permission to play every day and remember that play can simply mean talking to your dog or it can be reading aloud works of literature to your partner.

> **B** For instance, he found that lack of play was just as important as other factors in predicting criminal behavior among people in Texas prisons. He also discovered that playing together helped couples strengthen their relationship and sometimes reignite feelings for each other they thought they had lost.

> **C** In his book, *Play*, author and psychiatrist Stuart Brown, MD, compares play to oxygen. He writes, "... it's all around us, yet goes mostly unnoticed or unappreciated until it is missing." This might seem surprising until you consider everything that constitutes play. "Play is art, books, movies, music, comedy, and daydreaming," writes Dr. Brown.

> **D** You could also surround yourself with playful people. Both Brown and White stressed the importance of selecting friends who are playful—and of playing with your loved ones.

> **E** They suggested that play can be both spontaneous and planned. Their book gives examples of adults who created play days, not for their children, but for themselves and their adult friends and neighbors. They had all the kinds of things you'd expect to see at a children's party but without the children.

> **F** Today, White continues to clown at children's hospitals and orphanages all over the world. He even clowns at corporate presentations and prisons. "Clowning isn't something we're doing with kids, we clown with everybody," he said.

> **G** In Colombia, White's wife and Patch Adams's son—also clowns—visited a bedridden father, at his daughter's request. Once there, they sat on either side of his bed. He didn't know English, and they didn't know Spanish, but still, they sang songs, laughed, and played with a whoopee cushion. They also cried. The woman later told them that her father deeply appreciated the experience.

**D You see the following announcement in an international magazine.
Write your competition entry in 220 to 260 words.**

> **BEST CHILDREN'S GAME COMPETITION**
> We are making a TV program about the best children's games around the world.
> Which game would you like to nominate to be included in the program? Write and
> tell us what the game is, how it's played, and why it should be included.

UNIT 10 FACT OR FICTION

1 VOCABULARY: falsehood

A Complete the collocations with words from the box. Use the definitions to help.

> fake   gullible   hoax   misconception   myth   phony

synonym	word + collocation
1 mistaken belief or opinion	popular/common _____
2 not genuine	_____ passport/fur
3 trick; deception	bomb/elaborate _____
4 naïve; too trusting	_____ tourists/fool
5 fraudulent (person); not real	_____ explanation/British accent
6 fiction	urban/Greek _____

B Complete the blog with words from Exercise A. There is more than one correct answer for two of the blanks.

SCIENCE NEWS   HEALTH   SCIENCE   ENVIRONMENT   TECHNOLOGY   SPACE

In Defense of Old Wives' Tales   4:26 October 1

A widely held belief that lacks any scientific evidence to support it is sometimes known as an "old wives' tale." So, it would be natural to assume that old wives' tales were just for **(1)** _____ fools, right? Well, it turns out some are true. "An apple a day keeps the doctor away," is not a **(2)** _____ claim after all. Not only do apples help prevent heart disease and some cancers, but they are also full of vitamins and taste good! And how about "Starve a fever, feed a cold"? Until now, the common **(3)** _____ has been that this saying is nothing more than a **(4)** _____. But Dutch scientists have found that eating a meal boosts the type of immune response that destroys the viruses responsible for colds, while not eating stimulates the response that tackles the bacterial infections responsible for most fevers. Good news!

Bad news about carrots, though. They can't help you see in the dark—it was an elaborate **(5)** _____ which came about during the Second World War. And most of us still believe this **(6)** _____ story to be true.

---

2 GRAMMAR: inversion with negative expressions

A Underline the mistakes in the following sentences. Rewrite each sentence correctly.

1 Never I have met such gullible people. Tricking them was too easy!

_____

2 The tourist handed over his credit card, but little he knew it was all a hoax to get his money.

_____

3 Only when do you start to look into these conspiracy theories do you realize how crazy some of them are.

_____

4 Not only does the story be completely fake, it's also offensive to the people mentioned in it.

_____

5 No sooner had he read the article when he shared the link on his Facebook page.

_____

> ### WATCH OUT!
>
> ⊗ Little I did know, it was all a scam.
>
> ✓ Little _____, it was all a scam.

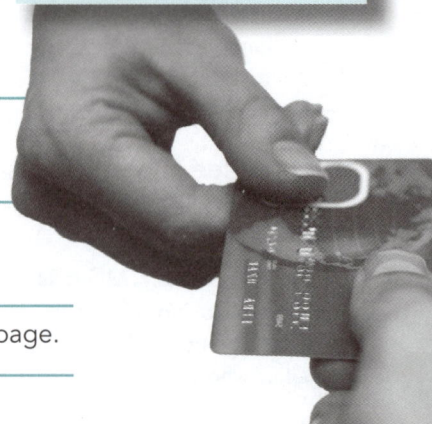

B Complete the sentences with the correct negative expression.

| Barely | Never | No sooner | Only when | Under no circumstances |

1 _____ you read it yourself will you understand how far-fetched it is.
2 _____ had he written the wiki article when it was edited by someone else.
3 Watching TV makes your eyesight worse? _____ have I heard such nonsense!
4 _____ will you click on that link—I'm certain it will take you to a phony website.
5 _____ was the claim made than the Snopes website debunked it.

3 VOCABULARY: word forms (proving and disproving)

A Complete the words in the email with the correct ending.

To: joshparks@macmillan.mail ✕ Send ✉

Dear Josh,

How are you? I'm doing great—I only wish I could say the same about Ben. He's taken all this stuff with the college pretty hard. He's actually going to bring a lawsuit against the college for wrongful **(1)** dismis_____. And it looks like the evidence **(2)** valid_____ his claim. It'll be interesting to hear what the dean says. Guess what? I had **(3)** verifi_____ that my scholarship has been approved, which is great news. They **(4)** confir_____ it last week. I know what I wanted to tell you about. I read an article **(5)** debun_____ the myth about the modern image of Santa Claus being created by a soft drink company. Do you remember that TV show we saw which **(6)** supp_____ it? Well, this article totally **(7)** disprov_____ it. It shows pictures of the modern Santa that pre-dated those pictures. Dumb TV show!

Anyway, write me soon,
Will

4 LISTENING: difficult situations

A ») 17 Match each phrase (1–8) with the more rapid way of saying it (a–h). Listen to the conversation and check the words you hear.

1 __ don't know	5 __ got to	a) wanna	e) whaddaya
2 __ going to	6 __ want to	b) lemme	f) kinda
3 __ what do you	7 __ should have	c) dunno	g) gotta
4 __ kind of	8 __ let me	d) gonna	h) shoulda

B Listen again. Choose the correct options to complete the phrases that Joe uses for clarification.

1 *What* / *How* do you mean *of* / *by* "verified the data"?
2 Sorry, *can* / *could* you say that *again* / *twice*?
3 *Pardon* / *Sorry*, she'll *what* / *say*?
4 *You've* / *You'd* lost me.

C Listen again and choose the correct option to complete the sentences.

1 Kenny *likes* / *doesn't like* Joe's article.
2 Joe *has* / *hasn't* verified the facts in his article.
3 Kenny thinks the professor *will* / *won't* be impressed with Joe's work.
4 Joe is going to check his work against *Wikipedia* / *his home encyclopedia*.
5 Kenny says you catch a cold if you *don't wear enough* / *come into contact with a virus*.
6 Joe *thinks* / *doesn't think* hair grows back stronger after it's cut.
7 Joe *can* / *can't* spell "appendix."

5 WRITING: a wiki entry

A Read the wiki article about a haunted house. Circle and correct the four grammar, two spelling, and two punctuation mistakes.

HOME	NEWS	PICTURES	FORUM	COMMUNITY

Haunted House

Borley Rectory was builded in east America on 1963 by Reverend H. D. Bull. It was a small house surounded by trees. At first, not only is the ghost of a nun seen, but also shadowy figures were spotted in the garden. However, the ghosts were not violent. Six years later, william Price, who was the owner, reported poltergeists in the house. Price burned the hosue down and then tried to collect insurance money, but he didn't get it. the house is gone now, but the legend has never been completely disproval.

B Read these two extracts. Underline and correct the six factual mistakes in Exercise A.

> Borley is a small and remote village a couple of miles from the market town of Sudbury in Essex, near the east coast of England. When Reverend H. D. Bull built his rectory there in 1863, it dominated the surrounding area. It was a huge mansion with 11 bedrooms and extensive attics and cellars with many staircases, surrounded by tall trees.
> At first, the apparitions were distinctly stereotypical in nature. A ghostly nun was seen in the garden, and shadowy figures were seen in the children's bedrooms. In light of how the legend was to develop, it is interesting to note that no poltergeist activity was reported during this period. In fact, it wouldn't be until more than 60 years later when the first poltergeist was reported.
> *December 17*

A History of Borley
Over a ten-year period (between 1929 and 1939), celebrated ghost-hunter Harry Price investigated the paranormal activity in the house and supported the claims of the occupants. He conducted a series of experiments, which validated much of what had been said about the poltergeist activity in the house. Shortly after his experiments ended in 1939, the house was totally destroyed by fire. A man named William Gregson, who was the owner at the time, hoped to collect over $11,000. However, when they investigated the circumstances, the insurers dismissed his claim. Gregson wasn't the only one labeled a phony. Many have accused Price himself of being a fake. Today, Borley Rectory may be gone, but the legend lives on.

C Four of these sentences contain mistakes. Decide on the type of mistake. Write S (spelling), G (grammar), P (punctuation), F (factual), or N (no mistake). Where necessary, rewrite the sentence correctly.

___ 1 Borley is a quite village near the English coast.

___ 2 In 1939, the owner was Harry Price.

___ 3 Borley Rectory does not exist anymore.

___ 4 The owner was hoping to collect at least $11,000 in insurance money.

___ 5 The house was totally destroying by fire.

___ 6 Gregson and Price were both labeled, phonies.

6 GRAMMAR: ellipsis and substitution

A The conversation has several examples of ellipsis. Insert the words below to complete the full version. Each word may be used more than once.

| are you | do you | I | I'm | is it | is that | it | it's | that's | that was | there are | who is |

Katherine: Hi Marcos.

Marcos: Hi. What's up?

Katherine: Not much. **(1)** (___*I'm*___) Just doing some reading for Professor Watson's assignment. **(2)** (_____) Know the one I'm talking about?

Marcos: I think I know it. **(3)** (_____) All about conspiracy theories, **(4)** (_____) right?

Katherine: **(5)** (_____) right. I decided to present about a conspiracy theory, so I went to this website. Here, check it out. It's a blog **(6)** (_____) called "EverybodyLying.com."

Marcos: That sounds… interesting. **(7)** (_____) Useful?

Katherine: I don't think it is. **(8)** (_____) Seems to be something **(9)** (_____) written by a 10 year old. **(10)** (_____) Spelling mistakes everywhere, and the content is very unusual. Here, for example, he writes…

Marcos: **(11)** (_____) Sure it's a man **(12)** (_____) writing it?

Katherine: I guess I'm not sure. Anyway, he—or she—writes that Michael Jackson didn't actually die. Apparently he's alive and well and working for the CAI. **(13)** (_____) Guess he means the CIA.

Marcos: I imagine he does. Does he give any supporting evidence to validate this; references, links to other sites, that kind of thing?

Katherine: Well, I can't see any, so I guess he doesn't. **(14)** (_____) Just his own crazy thoughts.

Marcos: **(15)** (_____) Sounds like you'd better find a more reliable source for your presentation.

Katherine: I suppose I'd better!

B Rewrite the following responses. Substitute *so* or *not* where possible.

1 **Katherine:** Know the one I'm talking about?
   Marcos: I think I know it. *I think so.*

2 **Marcos:** Useful?
   Katherine: I don't think it is. _____

3 **Marcos:** Sure it's a man writing it?
   Katherine: I guess I'm not sure. _____

4 **Katherine:** Guess he means the CIA.
   Marcos: I imagine he does. _____

5 **Marcos:** Does he give any supporting evidence to validate this; references, links to other sites, that kind of thing?
   Katherine: Well, I can't see any, so I guess he doesn't. _____

6 **Marcos:** Sounds like you'd better find a more reliable source for your presentation.
   Katherine: I suppose I'd better! _____

IT'S NOT A CONSPIRACY THEORY, IF YOU CAN PROVE IT!!

WATCH OUT!

✗ Had you an email telling you you've won the lottery?

✓ _____ an email telling you you've won the lottery?

skillsStudio

APRIL FOOLS' DAY

A Match the words (1–10) to the definitions (a–j).

1	errand	a)	compliment (often insincerely)
2	festivity	b)	care for and help grow
3	flatter	c)	anger
4	gotcha!	d)	practical joke, usually at someone's expense
5	harvest	e)	joyful celebration
6	mock	f)	tease; make fun of
7	nurture	g)	journey to deliver or collect something
8	outrage	h)	turn
9	prank	i)	exclamation when you have tricked someone (informal)
10	rotate	j)	gathering crops

B))) 18 Listen to the podcast and match each country (1–6) to the information associated with it (a–h).

1	Britain	a)	a law was passed regarding songs on the radio
2	France	b)	a new calendar came into use in the 16th Century
3	Ireland	c)	doesn't have April Fools' Day
4	Mexico	d)	a tradition of sending people on meaningless errands
5	Switzerland	e)	a fast-food chain fooled its customers
		f)	still celebrates New Year in April
6	U.S.A.	g)	a news show ran a fake story
		h)	spaghetti was harvested

C Listen again and choose the correct option to answer the questions.

1 How often is the *Cultured* program broadcast?
   a) every day
   b) every week
   c) every 2 weeks
   d) every month

2 According to the podcast, why did the Mexican Government pass a law about music on radio stations?
   a) to help Mexican music develop
   b) to protect western music
   c) to protect the Ministry of Culture
   d) to spread Mexican music around the globe

3 According to the broadcaster, how should the podcast creators feel about so many people believing them?
   a) upset
   b) trustworthy
   c) incredible
   d) complimented

4   In which country might you be given an "April fish"?
   a)   the U.S.A.
   b)   Britain
   c)   France
   d)   Switzerland

5   What is the meaning of the broadcaster's final comment before ending the podcast?
   a)   Many people worry about being tricked.
   b)   A lot of people have been tricked before, and will continue to be tricked.
   c)   If you were tricked last week, it's your turn to trick someone else.
   d)   Only fools get tricked.

D   Listen again and complete the sentences with a word or short phrase.

1   In last week's podcast, there was a story about Mexican radio stations being limited to one _____ song per hour.

2   Thousands of listeners wrote in to express their _____ at such a law.

3   The podcast creators had assumed the listeners would look for supporting _____ from other sources.

4   _____ and practical jokes have probably existed since the beginning of civilization.

5   April Fools' Day probably began around _____, in France.

6   Before the Gregorian _____ was introduced, the New Year was celebrated at the end of March.

7   The April Fools, mocked by others, were those who continued to celebrate the _____ in March and April.

8   People in some places will try their hardest to _____ you.

9   A fast-food chain fooled customers in 1998 by announcing a _____ burger.

10   The left-handed burger is the same as a normal burger but all the _____ are rotated 180 degrees.

11   In 1957, the TV show, *Panorama*, fooled _____ of people with its story about a spaghetti harvest in Switzerland.

12   Hundreds of _____ people phoned the BBC to find out how to grow spaghetti.

E   Research a famous April Fools' joke or prank that appeared in the media (in a newspaper or online news source, on a TV show, or on a radio show.) Write a wiki article about it. Be sure to evaluate the reliability of any internet sources you use. Include references to your sources at the bottom of the article. Your article should include:

•   When it happened
•   Where it happened
•   Who played it
•   Who it was played on
•   Were many people fooled?
•   Were there any consequences?
•   Any other information you think is relevant

Write 200–220 words.

1 READING: understanding intent

A Read the article. What is the writer's intent?

a) To describe the financial implications of busking.

b) To persuade musicians to try busking.

c) To offer advice to potential buskers.

BY THURSDAY BRAM

For many performers who want to build a career, busking provides a way to get started. [1]Musicians like **(A)** *Simon and Garfunkel* and circus acts like **(B)** *Cirque du Soleil* got their start by busking. It works for almost any performer who can plan a version of their act for the street.

PLAYING BY THE RULES

[2]Before you start playing, it's **(C)** *crucial* that you learn the laws for the areas where you plan to busk, or you'll find yourself in trouble. Some cities allow unlicensed busking, while others require licenses. Events, shopping malls, and transportation systems can all have laws of their own, so research any place you think would be a good place to perform before you ever start playing. Make sure you get the appropriate licenses even if the process is a lengthy one.

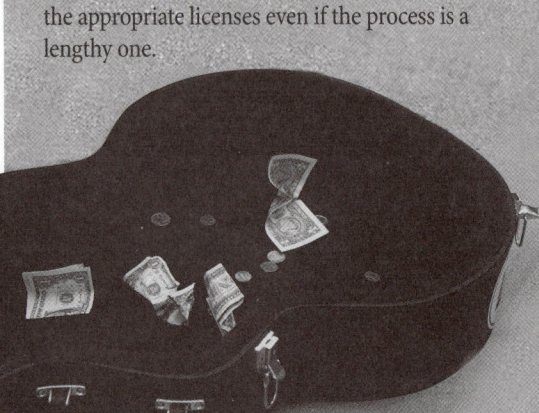

[3]**(D)** "PLAY YOUR SONGS, PLAY THEM WELL, EARN YOUR MONEY." GLEN HANSARD, MUSICIAN.

Buskers earn money from their performances in two ways. [4]The first is by collecting tips, or **(E)** *"passing the hat."* The second is by selling merchandise like CDs. [5]A good busker may be able to earn more than other available job positions, but you must remember that when performing for tips, **(F)** *"uncertainty is a dead certainty"*. [6]You can earn a dollar for an hour's performance **(G)** *(woohoo)* or you can earn more than $30 **(H)***(woohoo!)*.

It's also important to remember that busking requires skill. To be licensed to busk you will have to audition and show that you're capable of performing an entertaining set. [7]You may be out on the street and asking for money, but you aren't begging, or **(I)** *panhandling,* as it's otherwise known. [8]You're a **(J)** *performer*.

INCREASING YOUR PROFITABILITY

While busking, in order to increase your earnings, keep track of the details of each time you perform. Different places may have more generous audiences, or different types of performances may do better so that you can tweak your act and improve it. [9]It's a good idea to look for ways to increase, or **(K)** *"amp up,"* your connections with your audience. If you can add some audience participation to your act, you can increase your tips dramatically.

SO, WHAT'S THE BOTTOM LINE?

Busking can quickly become a way of life. Even if you start busking just as a way to move your career forward, you will find that there is a whole culture there and many great benefits. You can use it to travel the world, land bigger gigs, and make a name for yourself. There are even busking competitions so that you can see how you stack up against other street performers. Busking can be a big opportunity for anyone just starting out.

Adapted from www.investopedia.com

B Look at sentences 1–9 in the text in Exercise A. Is the intention of each one I (to inform) or A (to advise)?

1 ___ 2 ___ 3 ___ 4 ___ 5 ___ 6 ___ 7 ___ 8 ___ 9 ___

C Look at words/phrases (A–K) in the article and complete the statements.

1 Italics and/or quotation marks are used in _____, _____, and _____ to introduce a new word or phrase.

2 Italics are used in _____, _____, and _____ to emphasize the word.

3 Quotation marks are used in _____ to quote something someone has said.

4 Quotation marks are used in _____ to quote a phrase.

5 Italics are used in _____ and _____ to give examples of something.

6 Italics are used in _____ to indicate irony or sarcasm.

2 GRAMMAR: past tense for unreal situations

A Choose the correct option in the blog comments.

So, do you think you have what it takes to be a star?

COMMENTS

1 Paul91 6.31 · *What if / If* I could sing, I'd join a hip hop band and take over the world. Sadly, I'm tone deaf.

2 girlygirl 6.44 · *I wish / Unless* I were able to audition for Beyoncé. She'd see what a star I am!

3 MikeyH 6.57 · *Suppose / I wish* I were busking and someone from a record company walked past. Let's just say, I think they'd be impressed.

4 SaraPink 8.11 · *It's time / Suppose* someone realized I have what it takes to be a star. What's taking them so long?!

5 Catlover84 8.14 · I couldn't be a star *if / unless* I was in a band. I'm too shy to be on my own.

WATCH OUT!

(X) What if you have all the money in the world? What would you spend it on?

(✓) What if you _____ all the money in the world? What would you spend it on?

B Complete the comments with the correct form of a verb from the box. One of the words can be used more than once.

be   believe   get   have   if   suppose   time   unless   would

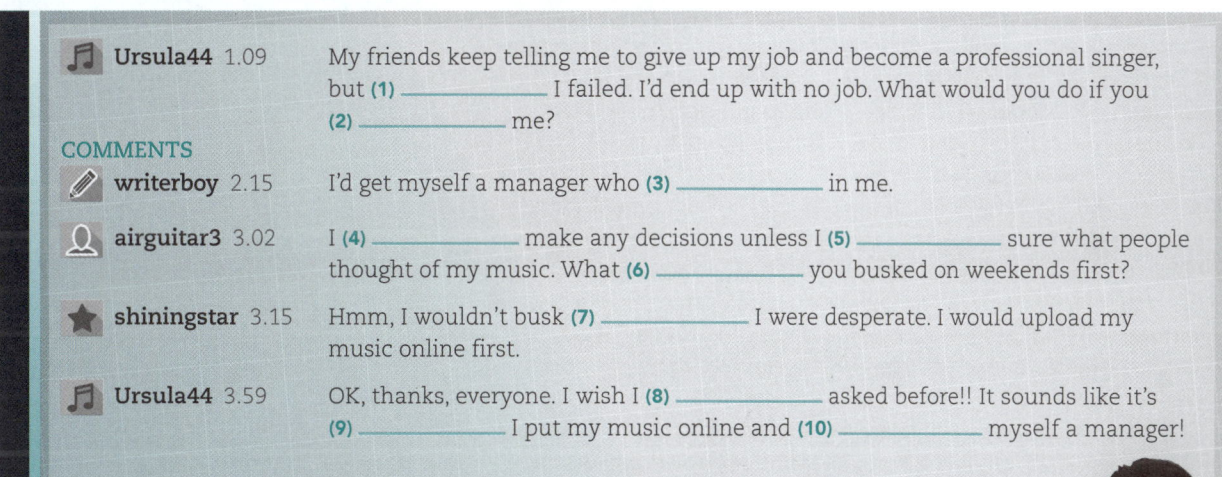

🎵 **Ursula44** 1.09 · My friends keep telling me to give up my job and become a professional singer, but **(1)** _____ I failed. I'd end up with no job. What would you do if you **(2)** _____ me?

COMMENTS

✏️ **writerboy** 2.15 · I'd get myself a manager who **(3)** _____ in me.

👤 **airguitar3** 3.02 · I **(4)** _____ make any decisions unless I **(5)** _____ sure what people thought of my music. What **(6)** _____ you busked on weekends first?

⭐ **shiningstar** 3.15 · Hmm, I wouldn't busk **(7)** _____ I were desperate. I would upload my music online first.

🎵 **Ursula44** 3.59 · OK, thanks, everyone. I wish I **(8)** _____ asked before!! It sounds like it's **(9)** _____ I put my music online and **(10)** _____ myself a manager!

3 VOCABULARY: idiomatic expressions with *take*

Complete the expressions with the words and phrases from the box.

for granted   into account   it takes   out of context   seriously

1 Not everyone has what _____ to be a street performer. You need both talent and charm.
2 It's hard to take street performers _____ sometimes.
3 Officials take a busker's skills _____ before issuing a permit. No one wants to hear bad music.
4 Most passers-by take street musicians _____ and don't bother to listen.
5 The mayor was quoted as saying he disliked buskers, but later said his words had been taken _____.

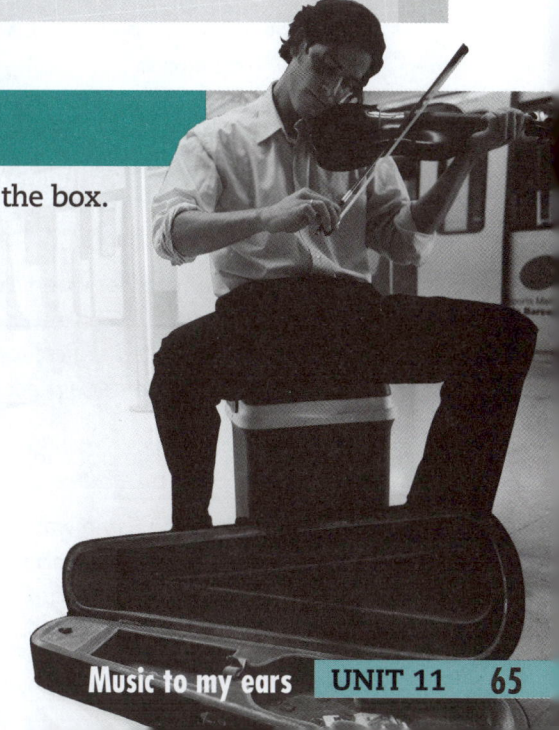

A Put the words in the correct order to form cleft sentences about Lady Gaga.

1 ~~it~~ / produced / Rob Fusari / who / her / was / early songs / .
It _____

2 ~~New York~~ / she / where / 20 years / lived / was / the place / for / .
New York _____

3 why / divides opinion / is / she / reason / because of / her dress sense / ~~the /~~ .
The _____

4 the year / she / when / was / her first album / ~~2008~~ / released / .
2008 _____

5 her / her contemporaries / that / is / distinguishes / ~~musical integrity~~ / her / the thing / from /
Musical integrity _____

6 was / on / *Telephone* / sang / ~~it~~ / her hit / Beyoncé / who / .
It _____

> ## WATCH OUT!
>
> (X) It was her mother inspired her to start singing.
>
> (✓) It was her mother _____ her to start singing.

B Read the text about Lady Gaga. Choose the correct option in each sentence. Complete the sentence with information from the text.

LADY GAGA

Lady Gaga was born Stefani Germanotta in New York City in 1986. A musical prodigy, she taught herself to play the piano at the age of four. **(1)** When she was growing up, she was influenced by Michael Jackson and Madonna. She continued to develop quickly and **(2)** she wrote her first song in 1999. She was just 13 years old. Then **(3)** NYU's prestigious Tisch School of Arts offered her a place when she was just 17. However, she left early to pursue her career. A producer who helped her write some of her early songs, Rob Fusari, named her Lady Gaga, saying **(4)** she got the name because she sounds like Freddie Mercury. According to Fusari, Gaga shares vocal similarities with Queen front man Mercury, who once sang *Radio Ga Ga*. What started as a joke between the two ended up as her performing name.

She was just 22 when she released her first album. **(5)** *The Fame*, released in 2008, launched her career and spawned a massive number one hit, *Poker Face*. By 2010, she had Beyoncé singing on what would be her fourth number one single, *Telephone*. **(6)** Lady Gaga now lives in Los Angeles and continues to divide opinion, with some openly critical about her dress sense and lifestyle, but **(7)** most people admire Lady Gaga's dedication to her art.

1 The people *influenced her when* / *who influenced her when* she was growing up were _____ and _____.

2 The year that *she wrote her first song* / *her first song was wrote* was _____.

3 It was *NYU that offered her a place* / *her a place that NYU offered* when she was just _____.

4 The reason *why was she got the name* / *why she got the name was* because she sounded like _____.

5 It *was The Fame* / *The Fame was*, released in _____, that launched her career.

6 The place where *lives Lady Gaga now* / *Lady Gaga now lives* is _____.

7 The thing *that most people admire is* / *which admire most people is* Lady Gaga's _____.

5 COMMUNICATION STRATEGY: softening language for refusals

A Complete the replies with the words from the box.

> honest   just   kind   know   opinion   really   sorry   sure   thing

"Would you like to download this song?" "I don't **(1)** _____. The **(2)** _____ is, I'm not sure it's legal."

"Can you share that file with me?" "I'm not **(3)** _____. It's **(4)** _____ that, it would be against copyright."

"Could you lend me that CD so I can copy it?" "I'm **(5)** _____, but I **(6)** _____ can't." "I think it's **(7)** _____ of wrong."

"Let's upload this song for others to listen to." "To be **(8)** _____, I don't agree with file sharing."

"Why don't we subscribe to this music site?" "Really? It's just my **(9)** _____ but it doesn't look very safe."

B 🎧 19 **Listen to a conversation. Check the reasons Amy gives for refusing Steve's request.**

1   She needs more information.   ☐   3   She can't afford it.   ☐
2   She thinks it's illegal.   ☐   4   She wouldn't use it enough.   ☐

C **Listen to the conversation again. Choose the phrase Amy uses in each sentence.**

1   *I'm not sure* / *I don't know*. I don't know how much I'd listen to it.
2   *It's just that* / *To be honest,* I'd prefer to wait because I don't know enough about it.
3   I don't know. *It's just that* / *The problem is* I don't really have the money to spare for it right now.
4   *I'm sorry, but I really can't.* / *I don't know.* Why don't you go ahead and subscribe though?
5   *It's just my opinion, but* / *The thing is,* I just don't listen to enough music to make it worth it.

6 VOCABULARY: sharing music

A **Put the letters in the correct order to form words about sharing music.**

1   itchgopry   _____   4   acrypi   _____
2   arctk   _____   5   elif ghirasn   _____
3   tamres   _____   6   cribbuses   _____

B **Complete the blog with the words from Exercise A.**

my**Blog**

| By Sarah / April 6 / 5 comments | add comment | forum |

There are some well-known websites that allow you to **(1)** _____ just about all the music you can think of—for free. You don't need to worry about **(2)** _____ as the activity on these sites is sanctioned by the music industry. So, royalties are paid on all music played, and the **(3)** _____ is protected; plus there's less need for illegal **(4)** _____ among listeners. However, they aren't perfect. You usually have to put up with random ads unless you **(5)** _____ to the Premium option and pay a monthly fee. And some musicians claim the royalties they receive are much smaller than they would get from the sale of a **(6)** _____.

Key trends   Channels   International   blogs
Top topics   Reports   chat room   my account

skillsStudio

A Read the blog on page 69. What reasons does the writer give for the increased popularity in vinyl records? Check all possible answers.

1. ☐ art work
2. ☐ online advertising
3. ☐ piracy
4. ☐ sense of community
5. ☐ sound quality
6. ☐ type of music

B Read the blog in Exercise A again. Find words/phrases which mean the following.

1. the start of something again which quickly increases in influence, effect, etc.
   (paragraph 1) _____ (n.)
2. better than something else in quality
   (paragraph 3) _____ (adj.)
3. the form that a movie, television program or music recording, etc. is produced in
   (paragraph 3) _____ (n.)
4. people or groups with similar tastes and interests
   (paragraph 6) _____ (adj.)
5. something that is excellent and admired by a lot of people
   (paragraph 6) _____ (n.)
6. something personal or private that you say or do
   (paragraph 9) _____ (n.)

C Choose the correct option, a, b, c, or d to answer the questions.

1. Vinyl records are …
   a) selling faster than downloaded music.
   b) following a different trend than CDs.
   c) seeing lower sales than a decade ago.
   d) losing sales to music streaming sites.
2. What does the writer say about the quality of sound in different formats?
   a) Some people believe that vinyl records are of the same or higher quality than CDs.
   b) The audio on modern vinyl is exactly the same as when it was captured.
   c) Digital recordings reflect the sound made when it was first recorded.
   d) Most people can recognize the accuracy of sound on a record.
3. People in record shops …
   a) have a vague interest in differing types of music.
   b) want to reproduce the experience of listening at home.
   c) are hoping to make copies of albums to sell on to others.
   d) enjoy being able to physically touch the albums.
4. What does the writer say about music and art?
   a) There is a new connection between the two things.
   b) Artists create album covers so they can be displayed.
   c) Art is just as attractive on the cover of a CD.
   d) It is common for people to buy records for the art.
5. What does the writer believe about the act of playing a record?
   a) It provides a stronger link to the music.
   b) It ties you to the room you are in.
   c) It gives you a longer listening experience.
   d) It takes too much time to organize.
6. What possible reason does the writer give for young people buying records?
   a) Young people have become interested in things from the past again.
   b) Music sold on vinyl appeals only to the younger generation.
   c) Records display music better than on other formats.
   d) Teenagers want to connect with each other through records.

Why is vinyl
BECOMING POPULAR? *By Lucas Kiss*

[1]Vinyl records are experiencing a global resurgence. Sales are the highest they have been in 15 years. Figures show the industry is booming, with 2.9 million records sold in the past 6 months—a 33.5% rise in sales over the first half of the year.

[2]Comparatively, CDs are still struggling with sales falling another 14%, as digital music continues to rise as expected—mostly due to the success of music streaming services such as Spotify. So what is causing vinyl to succeed when other physical media is not?

[3]One reason is that many audiophiles believe the sound quality of vinyl records is superior to other formats. By definition, original sound is analog. CDs and MP3s are digital recordings while vinyl records are analog recordings. Digital recordings take images of the analog signal at a certain rate (44,100 times a second for CDs) and measure each image with certain accuracy dependent on how many bits its format is.

[4]So basically, rather than capturing the complete soundwave, digital recordings approximate it into a series of steps. The bad thing about this is, it causes digital recordings to lose some information in the process. In contrast, vinyl records have tiny grooves—or lines—cut into them that capture the entire soundwave of the original recording. This prevents any information from being lost during the recording process.

[5]This may sound too good to be true, and it usually is, since most modern albums are recorded digitally before being pressed on vinyl. However, many audiophiles make the claim that the quality is still equal to or even better than that of a CD.

[6]As well as the audio benefits of buying a vinyl album, there is also a feeling of community when walking into a record store and being surrounded by like-minded individuals all digging through boxes trying to find a jewel. Unlike iTunes and Amazon, record stores are a place where people with many diverse music tastes can gather and share their musical tastes with each other in person. They are marketed towards music lovers, and through being so hands on, they do quite a great job.

[7]Vinyl albums are also almost impossible to pirate, which must appeal to the record companies.

[8]Visual art also explains the growth of vinyl. Music and visual art have also been strangely linked ever since album covers were invented. The large covers and glossy finish of vinyl records provide a large canvas for album art. Many artists take advantage of this, and there is no doubt that many people purchase records simply for the visual beauty they contain. They just look so much prettier than CDs.

[9]There is also a level of intimacy in playing a record. To play one, you have to physically set up the record player, clean dust off it, put it on the record player, and stay close to it so you can turn it over to the other side when it finishes playing. This gives listeners an intimate listening experience. It allows you to feel as though you are a part of the music you are listening to. You feel connected to the music and rewarded for the effort you put in to make it play.

[10]Of course most modern albums available on vinyl come with a free MP3 download. This gives listeners the convenience of not always having to be around their record player whenever they want to listen to the album they bought. They are also quite reasonably priced, coming in between $15 and $30 for a new release, and many good quality second-hand records sell for under $10.

[11]The top 5 vinyl record sales at the time of writing are albums which suggest a young demographic is mainly purchasing vinyl records. This could be due to an increase in the popularity of things from earlier decades, or it could be because some young people feel disconnected with music you cannot touch, as it is presented digitally. Either way, young people are getting into records and this trend is rapidly increasing.

[12]It appears the increasing popularity of vinyl records is here to stay. There are a growing number of artists and record labels who offer promotional LP releases on vinyl. There is even a Record Store Day held every April, where stores worldwide celebrate everything record-related through giveaways, competitions, and promotions. It certainly seems that vinyl records aren't going anywhere any time soon.

Adapted from *techgeek.com.au*

D Read the advertisement below. Write between 220 and 260 words.

Red Box Radio Writing Competition
What are your two favorite albums of all time? Who made them? Why are they special? Write a review, comparing both albums and enter them in our writing competition.

UNIT 12 DOWN TO EARTH

1 GRAMMAR: participle clauses

A Correct the mistakes in the following sentences.

1 Lived for so long in such a cold city, he now wants to move somewhere warmer.
   _____

2 Now forgetting by most people, this quiet town used to be the center of trade.
   _____

3 He was alone on the island for 6 months, survived on the fish he caught.
   _____

4 Knew for its hot springs, Japan is rich in volcanic activity.
   _____

5 Get lost in the desert was one of the scariest experiences of my life.
   _____

B Complete the article with the correct form of the verbs from the box.

experience   fly   prepare   run   strike

The San Andreas Fault

(1) _____ over California, you can appreciate the San Andreas Fault in its entirety. The San Andreas Fault is a line of intersection between two tectonic plates. **(2)** _____ almost the entire length of California, it stretches for about 1,300 kilometers. Although geologists try to analyze activity along the fault for warning signs of catastrophic earthquakes, it is difficult to recognize the signs before it is too late. **(3)** _____ by a "big one" in 1906, San Francisco is right on the fault line, and some people there fear another huge earthquake. In fact, **(4)** _____ many earthquakes, some California residents have assembled "earthquake kits," **(5)** _____ themselves for future quakes.

2 VOCABULARY: adverbial modifiers

A Complete the adverbs with the missing vowels.

1 sl __ ghtly
2 __ sp __ c __ __ lly
3 s __ m __ wh __ t
4 c __ mpl __ t __ ly
5 t __ t __ lly
6 __ ncr __ d __ bly

B Choose the correct options to complete the online comments.

greenboy	California is **(1)** *slightly* / *incredibly* beautiful. I visited last year and fell in love with it. In light of the news of recent activity along the San Andreas Fault, talk of earthquake kits is **(2)** *especially* / *slightly* relevant.
jake2591	To read these comments, anyone would think an earthquake is imminent, when I think the truth is **(3)** *completely* / *especially* different. I find it **(4)** *completely* / *somewhat* surprising that even the so-called experts seem **(5)** *especially* / *totally* divided over when the next quake is coming. Personally, I prefer not to lose sleep over it.
ann395862	I hope that if Californians do see another "big one," it's **(6)** *slightly* / *especially* smaller than the one they had in San Francisco over a hundred years ago. Actually, I hope it's much smaller, for everyone's sake!

3 LISTENING: difficult situations

A 🎧 **20** Complete the two parts of phrases asking for repetition or clarification with the words from the box. Then listen and number the phrases in the order you hear them.

> did you say   many   on, I didn't catch that   say "Milan"
> that   you repeat that

1. ☐ Did you _____?
2. ☐ Hang _____.
3. ☐ Sorry, could _____?
4. ☐ What was _____?
5. ☐ Sorry, how _____?
6. ☐ Wait, what _____?

B Listen again and choose the correct option.

1. Suzy went to *Milan* / *Japan*.
2. Suzy went *diving* / *driving*.
3. She saw a structure that resembled a *temple* / *pyramid*.
4. It was first seen *25* / *75* years ago.
5. Suzy *thinks* / *doesn't think* the monument is manmade.
6. The structure is called the *Yonaguni* / *Origami* Monument.

4 VOCABULARY: geology

Complete the information with the correct form of the words or phrases from the box. Two words are not used.

> collide   crust   drift apart   earthquake   erosion   mountain range   plate   volcano

THE GREAT 1906 EARTHQUAKE

On April 18 1906, a huge **(1)** _____ measuring eight on the Richter Scale hit the city of San Francisco, causing more than $400 million worth of damage.
We now know that San Francisco lies on the San Andreas Fault, which runs through the San Francisco Peninsula into the Santa Cruz **(2)** _____. The San Andreas Fault is a fracture in the Earth's **(3)** _____, and on April 18, the **(4)** _____ on either side of the fault **(5)** _____ by six meters and then crashed back together. It was because these plates **(6)** _____ that the events of that day in 1906 happened.

5 GRAMMAR: impersonal passive in the past

A Complete the sentences with the correct form of the verbs from the box.

| cause | erupt | form | inhabit | leave |

1 This volcano is known _____ hundreds of years ago, but not since.
2 A supervolcano is believed by some researchers _____ the extinction of the dinosaurs.
3 Meteors striking the Earth are thought _____ many large craters around the world.
4 Humans are thought _____ the Australian continent for 45,000 years.
5 The Grand Canyon is said _____ by the course of the Colorado River, starting 17 million years ago.

> **WATCH OUT!**
> ✗ The volcanic eruption is said to inspire many local legends.
> ✓ The volcanic eruption is said _____ many local legends.

B Check the sentences that are correct. Rewrite the incorrect sentences.

1 ☐ An earthquake approximately 70 kilometers off the coast of Japan is known to cause the tsunami that struck Japan in 2011.
_____

2 ☐ The scientist is said to be falsify his data about the rock formations.
_____

3 ☐ The survivors of the earthquake were thought to have been trapped for 6 days.
_____

4 ☐ The Krakatoa volcanic eruption in 1883 was said to have been audible more than 3000 km away.
_____

5 ☐ The Arctic researcher is believed to dead when he got lost on his way to the North Pole.
_____

6 WRITING: an editorial

A Read the article. Choose the correct topic sentence for each paragraph.

> **ENVIRONMENT**
> Insulate the Glaciers

Paragraph 1 Topic sentence:
a) Glaciers, our planet's largest freshwater reservoirs, are under threat.
b) Wrapping glaciers in a blanket seems like a crazy idea.

____ Despite covering an area the size of South America, they are on the verge of disappearing due to global warming. This situation has undoubtedly been caused by humans, so surely it is humans' responsibility to solve it. To do just that, a pioneering solution has been proposed: the glaciers are to be wrapped in synthetic blankets the size of a football field to prevent the top snow layer and the ice below from melting.

Paragraph 2 Topic sentence:
a) There has been some controversy (unfair, in my opinion) surrounding the proposal.
b) It is not necessary to focus on the negative aspects.

____ First of all, some say that at $19.2 million per square kilometer, the material is too expensive to cover much ground. Secondly, people worry that it is impractical because it would be impossible to cover very much of the world's glaciers. Finally, there are many who warn against messing with nature, as there are always unexpected dangers to the environment.

Paragraph 3 Topic sentence:

a) There are few positives.

b) However, the positives outweigh the negatives.

> ___ It has already been trialed in the Swiss Alps and was found to cut down a staggering 80% of the usual thawing that would be expected on selected ski slopes. This is a sizeable reduction—we cannot ignore it when we think of the glaciers. What is more, the material is very strong and light, making transportation more accessible. Finally, it is environmentally friendly—isn't that the most important point when considering the future of the planet? Albeit on a small scale, I feel the ice-protecting blanket has a significant future.

B Underline the general issue and proposed solution in Paragraph 1, Exercise A.

C Read the article in Exercise A again. Answer the questions.

1 Is the second paragraph for or against the proposed solution? _____

2 How many points are presented to support this? _____

3 Is the third paragraph for or against the proposed solution? _____

4 How many points are presented to support this? _____

D When writing an editorial, there are a number of ways that writers can make their points more forceful and persuasive. Read the techniques (1–5), and write which ones are used in the sentences (a–e) below.

1 Use adverbs to show certainty and remove doubt:
"*the situation has* **undoubtedly** *been caused …* ", "**surely** *it is humans' responsibility …* "

2 Use adjectives that dismiss counter arguments, or emphasize points the writer supports:
"**unfair** *controversy*", "*a* **staggering** *80%*"

3 Include the reader by using "we", and tell them what they must and must not do:
"*we cannot ignore …* "

4 Ask rhetorical questions (questions that don't require an answer, but instead make a point):
" *… isn't that the most important point when considering the future of the planet?*"

5 Use the first person to show the writers feelings:
"*I feel*", "*in my opinion*" etc.

a) I don't believe that we can wait any longer before taking action. ___ ___

b) Don't we all want a better future for our children?
___ ___

c) This is definitely a measure that the government needs to take. You have to write to your local politician about it. ___ ___

d) The scientists wasted a shocking $5 million dollars on this pointless research. ___

e) It is together that we will overcome these difficulties. ___

skillsStudio

A Match the words (1–10) to their definitions (a–j).

1	adventurous	**a)**	exciting and interesting (informal)
2	off the beaten track	**b)**	to say what you think is wrong or bad about something
3	criticize	**c)**	the feeling of being very worried, disappointed, or sad about something
4	disastrous	**d)**	eager to try new or exciting things
5	dismay	**e)**	widely
6	diverse	**f)**	very impressive or beautiful
7	extensively	**g)**	if one person interacts with another, they communicate with one another and react to one another often while performing an activity together
8	hot	**h)**	causing a lot of damage or harm
9	interact	**i)**	far away from the places that people usually visit and are hard to get to
10	stunning	**j)**	having great variety

B 🎧 **21** Listen to the radio show. Match the locations mentioned (1–7) to the pictures (A–G).

1 Grand Canyon, U.S.A. __
2 Bali, Indonesia __
3 Ngorongoro Conservation Area, Tanzania __
4 Gobustan National Park, Azerbaijan __
5 Gran Salar de Uyuni, Bolivia __
6 Puerto Princesa, the Philippines __
7 Seljalandsfoss, Iceland __

C Listen again and choose the correct option(s) to answer the questions.

1 Which three sentences best describe Jonathan Bealing's thoughts?
   a) Mass tourism does have some benefits, which is why you shouldn't only try ecotourism.
   b) Tourists need to see more of the world, not just limit themselves to obvious locations.
   c) The planet we live on is amazing, and people should be willing to see more of it.
   d) Ecotourism doesn't solve many problems, and you should only go to places where there are no tourists.
   e) The radio show didn't present listeners with enough choices for their travel.

2 This is the … episode in *The Travel Bug* series.
   a) first
   b) third
   c) second last
   d) last

3 A 'bucket list' is …
   a) a list of places people should certainly see.
   b) a list of places to avoid.
   c) a list of places that are hard to reach.
   d) a list of places that most people haven't heard of.

4 Jonathan thinks that Bali …
   a) is a unique and original holiday destination.
   b) is an attractive location with an interesting culture.
   c) has too many hotels and not enough culture.
   d) isn't a good place to go on holiday.

5 Jonathan believes that …
   a) the show has not done enough to promote ecotourism.
   b) tourists should be more adventurous in their holiday choices.
   c) that everyone should visit Bali.
   d) that mass tourism is good for the local culture.

6 Why doesn't Jonathan think you should go to the Grand Canyon?
   a) It's not as amazing as everyone thinks.
   b) It's too expensive to get there.
   c) It's too crowded.
   d) It's off the beaten track.

Bucket List
- Great wall of China
- Grand Canyon
- Ayers Rock
- Niagara Falls
- The Pyramids

D Listen again. Complete the sentences with a word.

1 Jonathan believes Bali is blessed with a rich culture and welcoming _____.
2 If an area is not equipped to deal with many tourists, mass tourism can damage a region's _____ and economy.
3 Jonathan prefers to visit magnificent sites that he doesn't have to share with _____ of other tourists.
4 At the Ngorongoro Conservation Area in Tanzania, you might get to see wild animals such as _____, elephants and hippopotamuses.
5 Gobustan National Park in Azerbaijan is famous for its _____ volcanoes.
6 In Bolivia, it's possible to stay in a _____ hotel.
7 The _____ river in the Philippines is eight kilometers long.

E Research a location that is off the beaten track. Write an editorial-style review of that location, persuading readers why they should go there, and not to other more "traditional" tourist destinations. Remember to use persuasive techniques. Write 180–200 words.

Audio script

UNIT 1

Track 01

Claire: Mike, have you seen this ad for a clothes swapping party? I think we should organize one here.

Mike: Oh, er, well I suppose it could be fun. What is it exactly?

Claire: People bring clothes they don't want and swap them with each other.

Mike: Oh. Well, I guess it's an OK idea.

Claire: I'd argue that it's more than OK. It's great! People get new clothes for free and nothing gets thrown away.

Mike: Well you say that, but I'm pretty sure some people will just bring dirty, old clothes. And we'll be left with a big pile of unwanted stuff at the end of the night.

Claire: Oh, I tend to think people are a bit better than that. I went to a similar party last year and thought the clothes were more or less in excellent condition.

Mike: Hmm.

Claire: It seems to me you're not convinced.

Mike: Yeah, not really. But I'm willing to give it a try. It'd be nice to get all our friends together if nothing else.

UNIT 2

Track 02

1 Space must be so cool. Imagine being able to fly in orbit around the sun, float in gravity, and watch all those sunsets! Sometimes I actually *dream* of being docked at the space station and stepping into the space hotel. But I'll never have enough money to go. Even if I mortgaged my house in India and all my possessions, it would be impossible to pay the kind of price these space tourism companies are asking … I try to keep a positive attitude, though. Who knows? Maybe one day I'll be given the chance. I mean, it's not unknown for people to win millions on the lottery—even if it *is* highly improbable!

2 Space tourism …? To be honest, it doesn't really interest me at all. I don't know much about it, either. Everyone says a space trip would be incredible, but even if I had the money, I wouldn't go. I think the price that these companies charge is unbelievable. And I don't see why people are incapable of enjoying "normal" earthly things these days. There are so many ways to have fun and enjoy yourself on Earth! Like, camping under the stars in the Australian outback with my family is one of my favorite pleasures—you could argue that that is a kind of space trip in itself, couldn't you?

3 I would love to go on a space trip with my husband and children. We've been saving for years to go, but it seems improbable that we will ever have enough money. Unless the price is reduced, I don't see how we can manage it. Besides, right now they only offer trips for two couples, and I would like my children to experience the beauty of the great unknown. I couldn't possibly go without them! For now, we just keep ourselves happy by watching all the major events like eclipses, meteors, and comets, from the east coast of the US. But maybe one day we'll make it to space. I hope so!

4 I feel so excited. My husband and I have already made a reservation to take a trip with Orbital Inn. We've paid a 20% deposit of the full $4 million fee, and now we just need to wait to be accepted. It would be a lifetime dream for me and my husband, who is in fact an astronomer. Just imagine—we'll be in a hotel in space for three days, traveling around the world every 90 minutes and watching the sunrise about 15 times a day. I can't begin to describe how excited we are about it—even if it is a little expensive! I'd love to see England from space!

Track 03

Hello, and thanks for downloading this week's *Spaced* podcast. Let me start today with some questions: do you think you've got what it takes to start a new human civilization? Could you spend more than 200 days in a tiny space shuttle, with just three other people for company? Finally, would you be willing to say goodbye to your family, friends, and the life you've been leading?

These may seem like questions for a science fiction movie, but unbelievable though it may sound, this is becoming a reality. The Mars One organization is now recruiting volunteers to travel to Mars. You heard me ... Mars! The volunteers will set up a permanent human settlement and start the incredible process of colonizing the planet. If that doesn't sound scary enough, you haven't heard the best part yet ... this is likely to be a one-way trip! You'll be saying goodbye not only to family and friends, you'll be saying goodbye, probably forever, to your home planet.

This may seem like a very unattractive offer—since you might never be coming home to Earth, surely nobody in their right mind would volunteer. Well, that's where you'd be wrong. For the first round of recruitment, more than 200,000 people were inspired to apply, from all corners of the globe. This will gradually be narrowed down until just 24 candidates remain, who will begin eight years of training for the mission. It is hoped that the first four people will be sent by 2024, and shuttles with four more people will be launched every two years after that.

So, what does it take to be chosen to be one of the 24 intrepid explorers? According to Heidi Beemer, who has made it to the round two shortlist along with just over 1000 other hopefuls, her application highlighted her "adaptability, resiliency, curiosity, and leadership skills." These personal qualities surely are important although Mars One gives much greater detail about the type of person it is looking for. According to their website, future colonists must be able to make repairs (both physical and electrical) to the settlement, they must know how to grow crops in very small areas, and they must have a very good knowledge of personal health issues in case of any medical emergency. That is to say, colonists need to know how to mend broken bones, how to treat illnesses, and even how to take good care of teeth—after all, when you're about 50 million miles from the nearest dentist, the last thing you want is a nasty toothache! Unless you have these skills, you won't be chosen!

The sharper among you may well be asking yourselves: "But how on earth (pardon the pun) are they going to pay for this?" That's actually a very good question, since the project is not government-funded. Mars One is, in fact, a non-profit organization led by Dutch entrepreneur Bas Lansdorp, and the estimated price tag is ... wait for it ... 6 billion US dollars! Well, one of the key ways Mars One is looking to raise this sort of money is through private investment and sponsorship, but to generate enough, they'll really need to fire the public interest and imagination. One hope for achieving this is by making the whole event—from colonist selection, to training, to setting up the colony on Mars—a huge media event. That is to say, imagine a reality show where the contestants aren't fighting for a minor cash prize, but instead for the chance to become an interplanetary explorer. Imagine a show that locks contestants in a room together and then sees how they interact with each other while completing tasks. However, instead of mundane tasks in any old room, as we see in today's reality shows, these tasks will take place on another planet ... in order to stay alive. Sounds a bit more interesting, don't you think? And, if enough of the public invests time and interest in such a concept, then hopefully sponsors will invest enough money, and the project will be able to go ahead.

So, one more time: do you really think you've got what it takes to set off into the unknown and colonize the Red Planet?

UNIT 3

Track 04

1 A: It's amazing what information you can find about yourself if you look online. We can't keep anything private these days.

   B: Er … . Although I've never really thought about it.

2 A: You don't think anyone will put photos of us at that party on Facebook, do you?

   B: … I was supposed to be at work!

3 A: I wonder if young people will care more about privacy in the future.

   B: … It'll probably become part of the school curriculum.

4 A: Sharing everything online with everyone can't be good for society, can it?

   B: … But there must be some benefits or people wouldn't do it.

5 A: People shouldn't write anything online that they wouldn't want their boss to see.

   B: … It could get you into trouble.

6 A: One day no one will have any privacy. We'll walk down the street, store cameras will recognize us and send us a text telling us we can have a discount if we go into the store.

   B: Really? … It sounds kinda cool!

Track 05

1 Jane: Hi, everyone. So, we've got the rest of the afternoon to plan our group presentation for Friday. Why don't we start by discussing what we all learnt about privacy from our research? And then we can decide what our overall message should be. Who wants to start? OK, thanks, Danilo.

   Danilo: We often hear people say they "need their privacy." But what do they mean? Is it something physical, like having your own bedroom? Or something psychological, like the chance to be alone with your thoughts? Either way, according to my research, it's something that a lot of us consider extremely important. In fact, what I learnt is that in some societies privacy is considered a necessity.

   Jane: I don't mean to interrupt you, Danilo, but can you speak up a little? There's a lot of noise coming from next door. Thanks.

2 Jane: Well, that was really interesting. So, what was the next research topic? Oh yes … Is privacy disappearing? Your turn, Mike.

   Mike: Er, right, well, er, obviously, with the growth of technology, we're more connected than ever. This means that there's a lot of information about us online that other people can get access to. It's more difficult than ever to keep things private from companies and other organizations, or just friends or family. I buy something from a website and suddenly everyone in the world knows about it on my social network. My point is – privacy is no longer something we all enjoy in the same way our parents did when they were our age. I think we should definitely talk about that.

   Jane: OK, thanks, Mike. OK, um … Maybe we should move on to discussing whether this loss of privacy is a problem or not? Brad, that's you.

3 Brad: … So I think we should conclude our presentation by saying that we should be more aware of our lack of privacy, especially online. Because then we can make more informed decisions.

   Jane: Thanks, Brad. So does anyone else want to add anything before we start writing our presentation?

   Keiko: Yes, I agree with you Brad, but I wonder if we should come to a stronger conclusion and recommend a change in law.

   Jane: OK, a good suggestion Keiko. Sandy, I'd be interested to know what you think about this. You did some research about the legal aspects of privacy, didn't you? What does the law say about …

UNIT 4

Track 06

1 Our universities and colleges have always offered a broad range of practical subjects. But now we place even more emphasis on practical subjects. There is less interest in studying things like philosophy and sociology these days. People prefer more practical subjects like media studies, design, IT, and engineering. Environmental studies is popular now, too. And the other big difference is the connection to work. Before, only a handful of students did work internships. Now, almost everyone spends time with a company. I think it's excellent.

2　Over the last ten years, many universities in the cities have started to offer online distance courses to people living in the country. That's because there are still very few colleges in the rural areas. The online students can go to internet cafés in remote villages and study there. They can use their cell phones to contact their university professors if they are faced with problems, and of course the rise of social media—Facebook, and so on—has helped a lot. There is a higher drop-out rate, but I think that's because it's not always easy to stay motivated when you don't have a support network of like-minded students around you. Overall though, the ability to provide higher education to people who couldn't previously get a degree is a wonderful thing.

3　Our universities are top quality, with beautiful campuses and state-of-the-art equipment. We receive a very high level of education in a setting that reflects our culture and customs. The classrooms are connected to wind towers, which keep the interior cool. There are buses into the city and dormitories for the students who come from far away. Many of the professors come from other countries, so we are connected to the outside world and we all have a global outlook.

Track 07

Hi. I think everybody's here now, so let me begin. First of all, I know how busy you all are, so I'd like to thank you for sparing your time to listen to what I have to say. I promise to keep it short and to the point.

Now, I guess everyone has read the memo distributed by the college's management committee, but let me summarize it just in case. Put simply, the number of students at our college has been steadily declining in the past few years. Of course, this affects us by directly lowering revenue from students' tuition fees. However, there is another, more serious effect. The government has made it clear that over the next 15 years it wants to reduce the number of colleges and universities across the country. The way it plans to do this is by targeting so-called 'under-performing' schools; that is, schools that consistently do not meet their quota of students. If a college fails to meet its quota five years in a row (which we are in danger of doing), then the government will cut subsidies to that school. This will lead to a vicious circle, where we don't have enough students and we don't have the money to attract more students. In short, we are in a bad situation, and it's only getting worse. If we continue like this, we don't stand a chance of surviving.

This leads me to ask: why can't a college of high standing, like ours, attract enough students each year? Is it the poor quality of the education we provide? I don't think so; if that were true, we would have lost all of our students years ago. Is it our facilities? Again, I don't think so because we have recently upgraded the campus and we have state-of the-art equipment and modern classrooms throughout the campus.

The answer, I believe, is that we have failed to see that college education has changed, and more and more students are turning to distance education, or DE, to continue learning after high school. I'm sure you're all familiar with DE; I'm talking about providing education to students who are not actually here on the campus. They could be in another city, another country … a totally different continent even. Surprisingly, this concept is older than you may think—I believe the University of London started distance learning degrees more than 150 years ago—but the internet now allows us to reach huge numbers of potential students worldwide.

It's a win-win situation. Students benefit because they can learn however, whenever, and wherever they want. There's no need for the time, effort, and cost of coming to campus everyday, and the tuition fees are lower, so we can open up to students from whatever economic background. Of course, from our perspective, we get more students, more income from tuition fees, and we meet our quota so the government won't cut our subsidies. The college will be saved! Like I said: win-win.

Believe me, this is the way education is going. I've been trying to convince people of this for years, but until now my comments have fallen on deaf ears. Well, now that your jobs depend on this, I hope you'll be more willing to listen to me. And, if my words aren't enough, let me give you some statistics to help convince you:

More than 70% of colleges and universities now have online classes. 90% of community colleges have a website specifically to handle DE students. 71% of students believe that online classes give them more flexibility in their learning. And finally, one statistic stands out: since the year 2000, the market for online classes has grown by 900%!

We must not stand back and wait for students to come to us – *we* must be active in finding new ways to attract *them*. If we had adapted sooner, we wouldn't have gotten into such deep trouble.

But it's not too late. We don't need to make huge changes right away, just start to have a more up-to-date way of thinking. Let me now show you some ways we can incorporate distance education into our existing curriculum …

UNIT 5

Track 08

1 endangered species
2 wild
3 in captivity
4 smugglers
5 release
6 natural habitat

Track 09

The editor of the East Coast Daily believes that the wild animals which recently entered the city should not have been killed. Firstly, animals inhabited the area long before human beings. Secondly, we cannot expect to use their habitats—national parks—and not allow them to use ours. Their return makes the city more appealing and is also proof that we're taking better care of the city and its waterways.

UNIT 6

Track 10

Kate: Hey Mark, you're interested in robots, right?

Mark: Um, I guess, yeah.

Kate: Well anyway, you'll definitely be interested in this. It says here that robots of the future are actually going to be 'soft,' not the shiny metal machines most people imagine now.

Mark: They are?

Kate: Yeah, apparently. According to this article, researchers have already started creating robots made of supple material. By inflating and deflating it with air, the robot can change its shape easily, making it more adaptable than normal robots.
For example, if it needed to get into a small space, it could just release some air and slide in. And, they've managed to get these robots to move across some really awkward surfaces—even a hot grill! Cool, huh!

Mark: OK, whatever you say.

Kate: I don't think you're getting it, Mark. They're talking about getting these robots to move like worms or octopuses, and then maybe—some time way in the future—even using them inside the human body. Like, if you need heart surgery, they could send in one of these soft robots to do it for you. No need to cut you open!

Mark: Robotic worms performing an operation inside my body? And pigs might fly! What's the magazine, *Dreamers' Weekly*?

Kate: Fine! Don't believe it then! You really drive me crazy sometimes!

Mark: I'm sorry, I'm sorry. Come on, tell me more about these octopus-doctors.

Kate: Oh I give up!

Track 11

Jeremy Barker: Hello, and welcome to the *Tech Advances* podcast. I'm your host, Jeremy Barker, and today I'm joined by Dr. Julia Langham, an automation specialist at the robotics firm, Robotech Worldwide. Today we'll be talking about what's going on in the world of robot development. Dr. Langham, good morning.

Dr. Julia Langham: Good morning.

Jeremy Barker: Could you start by telling us a little bit about your work? Do you spend most of your time designing new robots?

Dr. Julia Langham: Not at all, no. Although much of the earlier part of my career was spent on actual robot design, these days I'm more focused on research. That is to say, my job is to closely study trends in technology and advances in the field of robotics. I then use that information and knowledge to suggest ways in which my company can develop the next generation of robots; ones that will benefit society and the human race generally … while making money for the company, of course—but that's just a fortunate by-product. The actual designing and building of the robots—that's done by a separate, very talented team of experts.

Jeremy Barker: I see. Now, in recent years, robots have become an increasingly familiar sight in our daily lives. What kind of progress can we expect to have in the next 10 years or so?

Dr. Julia Langham: Provided the funding exists, there is virtually no limit. Capabilities are improving by the day. For example, more and more police forces are starting to use robots to carry out their everyday crime fighting. They send robots into buildings where dangerous, armed criminals may be, and the robots inform the officers of the criminals' exact location. Some robots are also being used in war zones. One such robot, with a sensor known as "Fido," is able, like a dog, to 'sniff out' bombs before safely disarming them. No doubt, as the capabilities of robots grow, they will be able to offer even greater help to the military.

Jeremy Barker: Interesting. And what about medicine? It is said that in 10 or 15 years, significant improvements will have been made in the field of surgery using robots. Now, I don't know about our listeners, but I think I'd prefer to have a human in charge of any procedure that involves cutting me open. I'd be far too worried about a robot having some kind of malfunction. What would you say about that?

Dr. Julia Langham: Well, we are indeed in the process of producing genuinely innovative technologies for the field of robotic surgery. Personally, I believe that in 10 years, the greatest headway will have been made in the field of keyhole surgery, a type of minimally invasive surgery. To answer your point about trusting humans more than robots: no matter how focused the surgeon is on the job, he or she is still prone to slight movements, which affect the precision of the operation. But robots can be relied on to work more precisely. As robot technologies improve and become more user-friendly, more surgeons will attempt operations that they otherwise would not have tried. This is good news for patients.

Jeremy Barker: OK, but what about the downsides? People sometimes point out the ridiculous nature of certain innovations, such as cute robotic animals to act like your friend or pet. What's your response to that?

Dr. Julia Langham: Humans are naturally suspicious of anything that is new, but it's important to think of the wider implications. Sure, a robot animal that pretends to be your friend may seem funny. But these robots can actually pick up on your moods and feelings, and they can sense when you've had an accident, like a serious fall. Soon, they'll be able to check your pulse, blood pressure, and other vital signs when you hold them. With many of the world's societies facing an increasingly aging population, and with more and more elderly people having to live alone, just think of the possible benefits of this supposedly 'ridiculous' robot.

Jeremy Barker: I see. Fascinating stuff. Well, Dr. Langham, thank you so much for your time today.

Dr. Julia Langham: My pleasure. Thank *you*.

UNIT 7
Track 12

1 Food that's safe or good enough to eat.
2 Cheap enough for ordinary people to buy or pay for.
3 Designed to be thrown away after you've used it once or a few times.
4 Describes food that decays after a short time, especially if it isn't kept cold.
5 Describes waste material that can be changed and used again.
6 Can be separated into small parts by bacteria so it doesn't harm the environment.
7 Describes bottles or containers that can be taken back to the store so they can be used again.
8 Be in a position where someone can criticize you or ask you why something happened.

Track 13

Sam: Hi. How can I help you?

Mira: I think I have a problem. I can't stop shopping. I'm a shopaholic! It's getting so bad that I'm worried I'm not going to be able to pay my bills soon.

Sam: Are you in financial trouble?

Mira: Well, I'm not broke. That said, if I don't do something, I may be soon.

Sam: Tell me about it.

Mira: It all started with me buying myself something on the weekends as a reward for having worked so hard during the week. But gradually my visits to the stores became more frequent and, without realizing it, I became addicted. Although actually, I did realize it, but I didn't want to accept it.

Sam: Do you actually enjoy shopping?

Mira: Yes, I love it! Of course, having said that, I don't feel so good when I see my credit card statement. But I love the activity of going to stores and looking for something to buy on sale.

Sam: Would it be the same if you didn't buy anything?

Mira: No. But then again, I haven't tried that, so I can't say for sure.

Sam: Let's try this. Next time you go to stores, you look around, but buy nothing. OK? And then next time we can talk about it.

Mira: OK. Why not? You know, having thought about it, I don't see the point. Why go into a store if you know you're not going to buy anything?

Sam: All right, then. How do you feel about staying away from the stores? On second thought, how about trying to stick to an affordable budget first?

Mira: Yes, I've tried to do that but then something happens …

UNIT 8

Track 14

… and so on to the post-Impressionists. This piece is by Henri Matisse, one of the leaders of the Fauvist movement, their name meaning "wild beasts." The art critic, Louis Vauxcelles, named them Fauves after seeing an exhibition of their art. He found the style basic and unskillful. In many ways, Fauvism can be regarded as an early form of Expressionism.

The Expressionists were more interested in creating an image which contains the artist's own feelings towards his subject than an exact copy of what he was looking at. Look at this piece over here by Edvard Munch. The emotion practically jumps out at you. On the other hand, this work over here is by Georges Braque, who, together with Picasso, devised another movement, Cubism. Less emotion, more analysis, maybe.

The intellectual, but anarchic Dadaist movement arrived in 1915. Dadaism started as a reaction to the horrors of the war. You may have seen this work by Marcel Duchamp, da Vinci's *Mona Lisa* with a mustache and a beard. By disfiguring such an iconic work of art, Duchamp's aim was to make fun of— even ridicule—traditional art.

By the mid 1940s … another era, another war, and the center of the art world had moved from Paris to New York, partly because New York was safer than Paris. At this time, the Abstract Expressionists were emerging. Emphasizing texture, the artists conveyed emotions through the act of painting. This piece by Mark Rothko, who always denied painting abstract pictures, features large rectangles of color. Looking at it, I'm not sure how he could deny painting abstracts.

And, through here, Pop Art. It rose in the 1950s as a reaction against Abstract Expressionism, which was by this time an established school of art. Here's a series of prints from Andy Warhol. The Pop Artists were fascinated by popular culture, and through the use of everyday items, aimed to make fun of the traditional art world.

And through here …

Track 15

Dr. Bergmann: OK everybody—if I could invite you all to come back in and take your seats. Thank you. Now, before we start the Q&A session, let's just review the key points of this morning's lecture about art therapy. The potential healing power of art has been known for thousands of years, but it's only since about the mid-20th Century that it started to become a true profession. Put simply, art therapy is a way of representing thoughts and feelings— often psychologically troubling ones—through art, music, and the like. It can enable people to share deep, possibly hidden feelings and can also enable a profound connection between the patient and a trained art therapist; a connection they may be unable to make through words alone. A therapist can use this to help the patient understand their own personality, behavior, and issues they need to confront. So, should you have any questions, please feel free to ask them now. Yes?

Speaker 1: Er Dr. Bergmann, could you tell us what evidence exists on the effectiveness of art therapy?

Dr. Bergmann: Can I infer from your tone of voice that you believe art therapy to be pointless?

Speaker 1: Well, it's just that I sometimes wonder if the main aim of these therapies is to take money from people, rather than actually help them.

Dr. Bergmann: Now that's a very strong—and controversial—way of looking at it. Had any journalist or researcher found evidence to support such a claim, don't you think there would have been a huge scandal by now? There is in fact an increasing number of academic studies proving the value of art therapy, not only in allowing patients to learn about themselves. There is evidence, for example, that therapy helps cancer sufferers; it can help with depression and lower levels of tiredness, assist in dealing with pain, and improve overall quality of life. So please, don't be so quick to dismiss it completely. Ah, we have another question … yes?

Speaker 2: Dr. Bergmann, thank you for your lecture this morning. I just wanted to ask about the cost of art therapy, and how it compares to other forms of therapy.

Dr. Bergmann: A good question. If art therapy is not covered by your local health authority, or by your insurance provider, you will probably have to pay a therapist on an hourly basis—much as you would any other type of therapist. Depending on who you see, the cost varies a lot, but for some it can seem quite expensive. It also involves a large commitment of your time and effort. For these reasons, I would say that it's very important that people undertaking this type of therapy believe in it and in their therapist. Another question?

Speaker 3: Dr. Bergmann. It's hard to understand why art therapy is so popular given that so many artists have emotional problems.

Dr. Bergmann: Did you attend my lecture this morning? Anyway, this is where art therapy is rather misunderstood. The artists you're thinking of probably paint for a living, but are unhappy about themselves or some aspect of their lives. This has no bearing on art therapy. Look, it's important to understand just what art therapy is used for. It does not require you to be a proficient artist, but simply to use art as a means of non-verbal communication between you, the client, and your therapist. This is a great advantage for those people who have difficulty expressing themselves verbally. I think we have time for one more question before I move on.

Speaker 4: Would you say everyone could benefit from art therapy?

Dr. Bergmann: Not necessarily. If you are resistant to art therapy—perhaps because you don't really believe in its usefulness, and feel like you are wasting your time—then I think you would struggle to get any benefit from it. But that is likely true of any therapy. However, please remember this: there are people, many people, who enter a program of art therapy and develop a deep, understanding relationship with their therapist. Through this understanding they can learn more about themselves without ever having to try to explain. It is for these people we can say art therapy works. Well, it seems from your questions that some of you have at least a little interest in this subject, even if you aren't completely convinced by it. That's good to know. So, now I'm going to move onto a different subject: light therapy. Also dating back thousands of years …

UNIT 9
Track 16

1 **Hayden:** Hey, Phoebe.

Phoebe: Oh, Hayden, hi. I wanted to see you. I'm going over to the tennis courts later with Sam. We're going to get some practice in for Saturday's match. Are you up for it?

Hayden: Sounds great! But can I take a rain check?

Phoebe: Sure. Er, did I mention Max was going to be there?

Hayden: Really? Oh, I'd like to come, but I have to get home early today.

Phoebe: No problem. We'll have another chance on Thursday.

Hayden: Great! Maybe you could invite Max!

2 **Kara:** Hello?

Justin: Kara? It's Justin.

Kara: Oh, hi, Justin. What's up?

Justin: There's a special screening of a new French movie tomorrow night. Want to go?

Kara: Yes, I'd love to, but I have to babysit for my sister tomorrow.

Justin: Oh OK, no problem. Maybe next week?

Kara: Actually, what time does it start? I'll be free after eight.

Justin: It definitely starts later than that. Eight-thirty, I think. I can give you a ride, if you want.

Kara: Sounds great! See you later!

3 **Carly:** Hey, Nico. Listen, there's a new Italian place opening tonight. Would you like to try it out? I wanted to thank you for helping me over the weekend.

Nico: Are you serious? You're inviting me to a proper restaurant? Not just a fast food place?!

Carly: Yes, of course!

Nico: Wow, that's really nice of you, but sorry, can't do it. Not tonight, anyway.

Carly: Oh. Is there a problem?

Nico: I promised my brother I'd help fix his motorcycle.

Carly: So maybe next weekend?

Nico: Definitely.

UNIT 10
Track 17

Kenny: Hey, this is interesting stuff, Joe.

Joe: Thanks, Kenny. I didn't think you were going to like it.

Kenny: Like it? I love it! Have you verified all the data you've submitted?

Joe: What do you mean by "verified the data"?

Kenny: You know, you have to find independent validation for any facts that you present.

Joe: Sorry, could you say that again? "Independent …"

Kenny: Validation! Check the facts from other sources. Have you done that?

Joe: I don't know—I just copied it from Wikipedia.

Kenny: Wiki …? You can't do that. The professor will just dismiss it without reading it if she knows that.

Joe: Sorry, she'll what?

Kenny: Dismiss it … reject it … throw it out.

Joe Oh, OK. I have an encyclopedia at home. I can check against that.

Kenny: Good! I don't think this is right. You catch a cold from not wearing enough clothes. Did it say that on Wikipedia?

Joe: No, I guess I made that one up myself. Is it not right?

Kenny: No! A cold is a virus. You have to come into contact with the virus. And what about this? Hair grows back stronger after it's been cut? Where did you read that?

Joe: Let me see that. Oh, OK, I think I need to check that.

Kenny: You don't. It's just a well-known myth! Just take those out. Leave the rest in and check them against your encyclopedia. And maybe, you should have learned how to spell "appendix."

Joe: You've lost me.

Kenny: You've misspelled the word "appendix." You've spelled it with one "p."

Joe: Is that wrong?

Kenny: Yeah, but don't worry. I really like your article. It's just that you've got to check your sources; otherwise, it can be disproved or you could get in trouble.

Track 18

Hi, and welcome back to another episode of the *Cultured* podcast—your weekly journey into customs and traditions around the world. As always, I'm your host, Mia White.

Now, you may recall that in last week's podcast, we told you that the Mexican Government's Ministry of Culture had passed a law allowing only one English-language song per hour to be played on all Mexican radio stations. The reason for this, we reported, was to nurture Mexico's domestic music industry, and protect it from so-called "western" music that spreads uncontrollably around the globe.

Well, rarely have we had such a response from our listeners. No sooner had the podcast gone out than you wrote to us in thousands, expressing outrage that they would dare pass such a law. It goes against freedom of speech, you said, against freedom of expression, and is a step toward the death of true culture. As a matter of fact, we couldn't agree more. However, we really thought that our good listeners, on hearing such an unbelievable story, would seek out further proof. We thought the whole thing would have been debunked minutes after the podcast went live. I guess we should feel flattered that our listeners place such trust in us that they believe our stories, no matter how incredible, without feeling the need for supporting evidence from other sources.

The truth is … there is no Mexican Ministry of Culture—at least not with that name—and there certainly is no law limiting English-language songs. We made it all up—it was just a hoax! If you check the date of last week's podcast, it was recorded on April 1 … April Fools' Day. Gotcha!

Pranks, practical jokes, and hoaxes have likely been around since the beginning of civilization, but what about this tradition of fooling people on one particular day of the year, and why April 1? Well, there are different ideas as to the origins of April Fools' Day, but these days, the most widely believed explanation is that it dates back to 1564. In that year, France adopted the Gregorian Calendar (the calendar still most widely used today) and the New Year began on January 1. Previous to that, they had celebrated the New Year for eight days at the end of March, with the festivities finishing on April 1.

After the move to the Gregorian Calendar, some people continued to celebrate New Year's parties on April 1, and it is thought that these people became known as "April Fools," and they were mocked by others for continuing to celebrate the New Year at "the wrong time." Thus, the tradition began!

And, it continues today in many countries around the world, fooling or mocking poor, unsuspecting victims. In France, where the tradition was born, an April fool is known as a *poisson d'avril*, or "April fish," and people try to stick a paper fish on their friends' backs without them realizing. In other countries—I heard this one from an Irish coworker—you may be sent on a meaningless errand for hours on end, while in some places people will just do their best to trick you.

The media and large companies like to have their fun, too. On April 1 1998, for example, a fast-food chain in the US advertised their new "left-handed burger." It would be the same as their regular burger, they said, but all of the ingredients inside would be rotated 180 degrees. It may sound stupid, but apparently thousands of people went into the restaurants asking for the fake left-handed burger. And how about this one: In 1957, respected British current affairs and news show, *Panorama*, ran a story about a huge spaghetti harvest in southern Switzerland. The show even had a video of a family cutting the spaghetti from a tree and putting it into baskets. Totally unbelievable, and yet hundreds of gullible people phoned the BBC asking for the secret of how to grow great spaghetti.

So, if you were fooled by our story last week, don't worry. Not only were you not the first—you certainly won't be the last.

That's all for now. Have a great week, everyone!

UNIT 11

Track 19

Steve: Hey Amy, did you check out that music web site I told you about?

Amy: Kind of.

Steve: Well? What do you think? Shall we subscribe? It doesn't cost much.

Amy: I'm not sure. I don't know how much I'd listen to it.

Steve: Well, you can stream as many tracks as you like—it's unlimited. What do you say? Come on, let's do it!

Amy: To be honest, I'd prefer to wait because I don't know enough about it. It's a new service, right?

Steve: Are you worried about piracy? Don't worry, it's totally legal! You don't need to worry about copyright infringement or lawsuits from the music industry. Come on, let's give it a try.

Amy: I don't know. It's just that I don't really have the money to spare for it right now.

Steve: Suppose you borrowed some from me. Then it wouldn't be a problem.

Amy: I'm sorry, but I really can't. Why don't you go ahead and subscribe, though?

Steve: Sure, but if it's a money thing, you could subscribe for the basic service instead of the premium service. How does that sound?

Amy: The thing is, I just don't listen to enough music to make it worth it.

UNIT 12

Track 20

Suzy: Jack, hi.

Jack: Hey, Suzy! Are you back? How was it?

Suzy: I'm back, and it was amazing! It was totally different from any of my other vacations. You'll never believe it, in the end I went to Japan.

Jack: Did you say "Milan"?

Suzy: I said "Japan," not Milan. I went scuba diving in the south. I went on an especially interesting dive not far from Taiwan. It had this underwater structure, which looked like an underwater pyramid.

Jack: Sorry, could you repeat that?

Suzy: Sure. It looked like an underwater pyramid.

Jack: A pyramid? In Japan? Not a temple?

Suzy: I know! Weird, huh? Anyway, it was incredibly beautiful, and it was only discovered about twenty-five years ago.

Jack: Sorry, how many?

Suzy: 25, and not very many people have seen it since. And what I found a little surprising was that some people say it isn't man-made. They prefer to say it's a natural phenomenon.

Jack: And you don't think so?

Suzy: I can't believe that!

Jack: Hang on, I didn't catch that.

Suzy: I said I can't believe that. The lines are all too straight. Anyway, it's called the Yonaguni Monument.

Jack: Wait, what did you say? Origami Monument?

Suzy: No, no. Yonaguni Monument. There's even a book about it.

Jack: What was that?

Suzy: Jack, it's kinda noisy out here. I'm gonna call you later from home. OK?

Jack: Sure. Can't wait to hear the rest of it!

Track 21

Host: Good evening everyone, and thanks for tuning in to this, the last in the current series of *The Travel Bug*. Throughout the series, we've been presenting some of the hottest tourists destinations around the world, the places we believe should form part of anybody's bucket list—that is to say, the list of places to see before you die.

Well, today's going to be especially interesting because we've invited one of our less satisfied listeners. Criticizing us for only mentioning the "obvious" places—the Grand Canyon, for example—he has expressed dismay that we don't encourage our listeners to be more adventurous. Having traveled extensively himself, Jonathan has some strong ideas about modern tourism, and for the sake of balance, we thought we'd let him share his ideas on the air. Jonathan, welcome to the show.

Jonathan: Hi there. Thanks for having me.

Host: Now Jonathan, why don't you start by telling us what's wrong with people traveling to the island of Bali—another of our suggestions that you took issue with.

Jonathan: OK, let me be clear—there's nothing at all wrong with going to Bali. Blessed with a rich culture and welcoming atmosphere, it's a stunningly beautiful island. My problem is the type of mass tourism that exists these days, where people stay in large chain hotels, learn nothing about the local culture, fail to interact with their surroundings, and leave no wiser about the place they've just visited. What's more, this type of mass tourism has potentially disastrous effects on the ecology and economy of areas not equipped to deal with so many visitors.

Host: So you prefer some kind of low-impact ecotourism, where visitors learn about the local area and the effect their presence can have. A more respectful type of tourism, that is, that directly benefits the local population.

Jonathan: Well yes, I do agree that ecotourism is totally preferable to mass tourism, but actually, I thought you did a good job in episode three of explaining to listeners about ecotourism.

Host: Glad you think so. So what is it that you want to say today?

Jonathan: I want to push people to be more adventurous, get off the beaten track, and go out there and see the natural wonders that exist in all four corners of the globe. This planet we live on is completely incredible, and yet so much of it is unknown to so many people. Yes, the Grand Canyon is great, but millions of people go there every year. Why not go somewhere just as magnificent, without the need to share it with thousands of others?

Host: And I understand you've done just that. Could you tell us some of these lesser-known must-see places that you've been to?

Jonathan: Sure. How about the Ngorongoro Conservation Area in Tanzania, East Africa? Within it is an enormous volcanic crater (something like 260 square kilometers in size), formed by a huge volcano which is thought to have erupted about 3 million years ago. If that's not enough for you, perhaps you'll be interested to hear that hippopotamuses, elephants, lions, and many other creatures can be spotted there.

Host: You paint quite a picture. Anywhere else you'd like to recommend?

Jonathan: Well, staying on the theme of volcanoes, a few years back I took a trip to Gobustan National Park in Azerbaijan. It's famous for having about 400 mud volcanoes, formations that continuously give out a mud-like substance. Apparently the mud is good for your health, so you can join in with the locals and cover yourself in the stuff.

Host: That sounds … well, let's just say I don't think it's for me!

Jonathan: That's fine, it doesn't have to be mud volcanoes. All I'm saying is that there are so many natural wonders on this incredibly diverse planet Earth. The desert-like salt lake of Gran Salar de Uyuni in Bolivia (which includes a salt hotel, by the way), the jaw-dropping Seljalandsfoss waterfall in Iceland, the eight-kilometer Puerto Princesa underground river in the Philippines. Why be obvious and go where everyone else is going? There's so much more to see!

Host: I see. I'm afraid that's all we have time for, Jonathan, but I'd like to say thank you so much for coming and sharing your thoughts. Having heard you, I'm sure many listeners will now be somewhat inspired to venture farther afield.

Jonathan: It's been a pleasure.

Host: And that's all for this series—we hope you've enjoyed it. So, for now, goodbye.